# A KID ON
# THE COMSTOCK

# A KID
# ON THE
# COMSTOCK

*Reminiscences of a Virginia City Childhood*

## By John Taylor Waldorf

*Edited with Introduction and Commentary
By Dolores Bryant Waldorf*

AMERICAN WEST PUBLISHING COMPANY

PALO ALTO/CALIFORNIA

Portions of this book were originally published by the Friends of the Bancroft Library as *A Kid on the Comstock* (1968) and are used here by permission.

*Library of Congress Card Number 73-108628*
*ISBN 910118-14-0*

# Acknowledgments

*No one can find the way into a world so remote today as the Virginia City of* A Kid On the Comstock *without the guidance and interest of many. In research and in my later quest for photographs of scenes and people of the Seventies and Eighties as well as of John Taylor Waldorf's later career I am especially grateful to the staffs of the Bancroft Library, the Nevada Historical Society, the Nevada State Library, the University of Nevada Library, Special Collections, the Nevada State Museum, the California Historical Society and the Wells Fargo History Room.*

*Allan R. Ottley, head librarian, California Section, California State Library, has been of immense aid in solving knotty problems. Mrs. Andy Welliver, acting director of the Nevada Historical Society, Dr. John Barr Tompkins of the Bancroft Library and Lee Burtis, in charge of photographs for the California Historical Society, gave a great deal of time and thought in assistance. My very good friends, Mrs. Helen S. Giffen and Mrs. Ellen H. Dempsey were of priceless aid on two different safaris to Virginia City, in sleuthing out the sites of various places mentioned in the recollections.*

*Warm thanks to Miss Thelma Neaville of the Marysville Library, Roy D. Graves of the Society of California Pioneers, Walter Mulcahey, history buff of Reno, Nevada, Mrs. Vivian*

*Lyons Moore, historian of Hillsdale College, Michigan, and Mrs.
Morris Waldorf of Richmondville, New York.*

*To my two brothers I say thank-you once more: Howard V.
Waldorf who was a bulwark of faith and encouragement over the
long haul and Wallace A. Waldorf, who interrupted great responsi-
bilities in remote parts of the world to recall details and comments
on several trips to Virginia City with our father.*

*Mrs. H. C. Hunter daughter of Oriana Waldorf (Osterman)
and Stanley J. Waldorf, son of George W. Waldorf, contributed
mementoes supporting statements later made in the biography. Patricia McCarthy, granddaughter of Minnie Alice Waldorf (Mc-
Court) searched through many cartons long in storage to come up
with a bonanza of pictures.*

*My thanks would not be complete even if three to whom I direct
them are no longer living: Mrs. Helen H. Bretnor of the Bancroft
Library; Mrs. Joseph McCarthy, daughter of Minnie Alice Waldorf (McCourt) and Frederick E. Osterman, son of Oriana Waldorf (Osterman).*

*Finally my most hearty gratitude to Dr. J. S. Holliday, who,
as chairman of the Friends of the Bancroft Library, rescued the
manuscript from oblivion in a remote recess of a file cabinet where
it had been shoved by a frustrated writer, and to T. H. Watkins,
whose enthusiasm and especially creative editorial abilities have
guided this book into print in both the abbreviated publication of
the Friends and now in this full dress affair.*

DOLORES BRYANT WALDORF

*To Midget*

# CONTENTS

# A COMSTOCK PROFILE

CHILDREN WERE SELDOM SEEN on the Comstock in the early days when Sandy Bowers was a millionaire and his Missus Eilly Orum, in velvet and furs, rode her shining victoria from the mansion in Washoe Valley up Gold Canyon to parade her elegance along Virginia City's C Street.

It was a wild world, with brawling and lawsuits and overlapping claims. Attorneys in high boots sported ready derringers while they made thousands in fees, and disappointed clients defied court decisions, fortifying their mining shafts and arming their miners with muskets.

The petticoat world was mostly those painted ladies from the little frame houses down on D Street, flaunting their silks and satins as they looked down their noses at the pale housewives and held hilarious court behind the curtains of the boxes in the opera house. Most folks agreed it was no place for a child.

But by 1873, the year the Big Bonanza arched black and glittering along the drifts of the Consolidated-Virginia, there was law and order. Hundreds of youngsters, most of them children of miners, swarmed over the sides of Mount Davidson.

Among them was Johnny Waldorf, a curly-headed menace to parental peace of mind, who arrived in camp that year at the age of three and lived in a boy's paradise until he was not quite sixteen. For in 1886, after a little more than twelve tumultuous years, he ran away to find the ocean he had dreamed about and somehow make a fortune. In no time at all, he was looking back

1

with the most tender nostalgia to the sage and the mountain and the town.

For the remainder of an adventurous life, never dull and never without high hopes—as tramp printer, newspaperman, political campaigner, government official, and corporation publicist—those years in Virginia City became a powerful counterweight to all that he saw and heard and learned. It was a perennial backdrop. Somehow the dreams that came true, the ambition realized, never could hold a candle gleam to the years in that Nevada mining town on the sunrise side of Mount Davidson. The mark of the town and the time remained with him all his life.

The kids on the Comstock in Johnny's time were a contentious lot—cocksure, reckless, bellicose, and without mercy. They expected of life the frontier adventures and excitement their hardy fathers had known, many of whom had fought in the Civil War, many more of whom had come from mines in other lands to try their skill in the deep and torrid drifts of the Comstock.

But when those kids of the seventies were roaming the mining camp, none could see that the frontier was fading. Too much of it still lingered. It was like a hundred bands thumping martial music night and day. They reacted to it from waking to sleeping in the way kids do when the band strikes up. They were more than ordinarily obstreperous, more foolish than wise in daring, and completely unpredictable. Their parents bewailed it, but Dan de Quille[1] of the *Territorial Enterprise* was of the opinion that the light, thin air of the town's more than mile-high altitude made them as healthy and lively as they were—full-chested, deep-lunged, and tireless.

Whatever they did seemed in reckless competition with the casualty lists of the day before. In winter they coasted down the steep cross streets of town through the thick, uncontrolled, and hurried traffic on C Street—on more than one occasion just making it under a horse's belly or zipping under a train of moving ore cars on the spur tracks below E Street—and most of them survived. They slid down the dumps after wet boards and beams that came tumbling over the tailings and took their lives in their hands almost as many times a day as did the men down in the hot vitals of the Comstock Lode.

But it was more than the sights and the hopes of the town, the continual expectation of another Big Bonanza any day, that made the kids the way they were. No one seems to have taken into account the tremendous thundering orchestration of sound that Virginia City made in daylight and in darkness.

There was not only the endless racket but a sense of tingling primal force as the very earth vibrated to the industry beneath the town and on the surface. No child could have helped responding to it. There were the great stamp mills, crashing and pounding near and far—from the Carson River up Gold Canyon and all across the eastern slope of the mountain. There were not only sixteen and twenty stamps to a mill but some with as many as sixty huge stamps, all battering away around the clock at the ore which came up through the continually steaming mouths of the shafts.

De Quille regarded the sound of even one sixty-stamp mill as reducing Niagara's roar to a mere whisper and told of noise so thunderous that men had to shout in each other's ears as if they were a mile apart.[2] Many a miner remained a shouter to the end of his days after a career on the Comstock.

Johnny's father, Jacob D. Waldorf, whose voice had deepened from a farm boy's treble to the boom of command during artillery service in the Civil War, gained even more resonance as a shift boss in mines of the Comstock and never stopped shouting in all his remaining years. It became his normal tone of voice.

But the stamps were only the drumbeat measuring the orchestration of Comstock sounds. There were the mine whistles, hooting each change of shift around the clock, shrilling an alarm of fire, celebrating the departure or return of a train of flat cars laden with picnicking children. There were the rumbling trains of ore cars, trundling their loads along the innumerable spur tracks on their way to the main line of the Virginia and Truckee —then rattling back empty for more quartz.

There were creeping freight trains, winding up the grade with supplies for the thousands in that mountain town. There were

the glorious Virginia and Truckee passenger trains, green cars
with varicolored window tops, red and gold engines and trum-
pet-mouthed Dolly Varden stacks, emerging grandly from the
last tunnel on E Street in the early morning and departing into
the night for Reno and connection with the east- and westbound
Central Pacific trains.

There were the omnibuses to Gold Hill, the carriages, the
shouting drivers, the nervous horses, the chunking of hooves,
the hullabaloo of a runaway team, the great freight trucks,
strung trailer style, dragged by as many as sixteen huge horses.
There was a constant mumbling, droning sound of men discuss-
ing stocks before the telegraphed quotations on the bulletin
boards of the mining brokers. There was something like the
pulse of the Lode itself, a vibration and throbbing, a shushing
sort of obligato as the great Cornish pumps down below sucked
the scalding water away from the levels where the fathers of
those kids on the Comstock picked and dug at the rock. And
above and around all those sounds was the rush and rattle of the
"zephyrs," the piercing, diving draughts and ruthless whirlwinds that swooped down the mountainside.

Johnny responded to that world of sound and sight and sense
as did all the other boys but with perhaps more imagination,
more awareness, more lasting emotion. So much did he respond
to the excitement and challenge of the Comstock that his homesick mother and his stern, purposeful father were often baffled
by their highly charged first-born son.

Johnny's mother, born in 1843 in Somerset, Michigan, was
just thirty when she arrived in Virginia City in 1873. She came
of New England stock, a long line of upright folk descended
from Thomas Slayton, who had migrated to the Colonies in
1690, a cabin boy at the mature age of eight years. The family
had lived quietly through a number of generations in East
Brookfield, Massachusetts, before the spirit of Thomas sent
sons in search of new and far frontiers. Elijah, Johnny's ma-
ternal grandfather, was born in Calais, Vermont, but he was
farming in Michigan when Johnny's mother was born.

She was the first child born to a middle-aged couple who had
both raised large families, been bereaved, and married a second

time. She was dearly beloved and probably gently indulged by her parents and her many half brothers and sisters. There is an old tintype of her, a pretty child, taken with her fond father who looked as if he could have been her grandfather.

She had been named Cynthia Adeline Slayton but had blithely and probably wilfully changed her name to Adeline C. by the time she became a school teacher in her late teens. She married Jacob D. Waldorf when she was twenty-one.

Jacob was a tall, sandy-haired, lean-featured artillery captain, who returned to Hillsdale on leave shortly after he had been commissioned in the field in Georgia. He visited Hillsdale College, where he had studied briefly before enlisting in 1861, and at some affair, one of the get-togethers of the rural community during that leave, he and spunky Miss Adeline met.

It was a typical wartime romance. Jacob was glorious in the dark blue uniform with knit cerise silk sash and flashing sabre when they were married in Hudson, Michigan, on January 25, 1865. They went back to his headquarters in Kentucky to spend part of their honeymoon. Addie thought it great fun when a guerrilla band howled in attack and bullets whipped and whispered around the tent and cut the canvas while she wrote dispatches for the Colonel. But it was soon over, and she was packed off back to peaceful Hillsdale.

At a distance the prospect of going to the Comstock might have seemed as exciting to her as the guerrilla raid, but Virginia City was a very different sort of place from what she had ever known. Addie was never cut out to be a pioneer. Her life in Virginia City was always temporary in her mind, something to be endured with as much patience as she could command. But once she had arrived, there was no escape unless Jacob could keep his promise to make a fortune and take them all back in glory to a bountiful dream farm in Michigan.

Addie's only escape from the drab hills and the rough ways of the mining camp was by way of the armloads of novels which Johnny lugged home from the Miners' Union Library. She loved the romances where the trials of the heroine ultimately ended in great and wealthy happiness. She was especially fond of Mrs. E. D. E. N. Southworth's novels. In time Addie became not only a client but a friend of Mrs. Lemuel (Sandy) Bowers, the Washoe seeress, and often visited her in hopes of being told just when and how that fortune would come to the Waldorfs.

Johnny's father was a man of deep, tenacious conviction. He did not smoke or drink, and he forbade card playing in his home. Addie was in agreement with his code, but she did think he was a mite too strict with the older girls, Minnie Alice and Oriana. Jacob, too, regarded their Virginia City stay a temporary one. He worked for but one goal, to clear enough on stock to take Addie and the children back to Michigan. For years he remained on the rolls of the local Masonic Lodge as "a visiting brother" from Michigan, where he was a Master Mason in Fidelity Lodge.

Neither of Johnny's parents approved of or could understand their eldest son's eternal sense of humor, a wit which would ramble on gaily with material at hand, with wry comments on himself as well as others, or stab like lightning at someone less willing to take it. The boy's outlook was probably an instinctive response to his father's driving zeal, so often beaten down through the years but never crushed by fate, the mining speculators, or the tribe Jacob referred to contemptuously as "the Capitalists."

Jacob Waldorf was born into the world of the Dutch and German farmers of Schoharie County in New York, not many miles from Albany. His Waldorf ancestors, whose path paralleled that of the luckless Palatines escaping from the tyrannies of Livingston Manor, had spent close to a century in rural contentment in Cobleskill and Richmondville before Jacob was born in 1840. His mother died when he was nine, and he left the county in his teens, never to return. He worked his way across the country to the Lake states and enrolled in Hillsdale College in southern Michigan. When the Civil War erupted, he enlisted in the First Michigan Light Artillery in December 1861, at the age of twenty-one. That was the end of his education by books, but it was not of his own choosing that he never returned to school. Life, as it often does, got ahead of him. His and Addie's first child, Minnie Alice, was born in December 1865, a few months after he had resigned from the army.

Farming was a dreary round of monotonous tasks after the

clash and crises of battle. In May 1871, he headed for the Comstock, leaving Addie, two little girls, and baby Johnny to follow as soon as wild Virginia City seemed safe—and he could send the fare.

With such parents—a former school teacher and a man whose efforts to gain an education had been cut short by war—Johnny was expected to excel, to stand at the head of any class. But it was the last thing Johnny wanted to do. His ability to keep school rooms in a state of snickers and turmoil appalled his father and mother. He was thrashed for it both at school and at home. His father always said there'd be a good larruping at home for every one he got at school. It was a promise faithfully and frequently kept.

Johnny apparently never made the slightest effort to win the approval of his teachers. He would have lost face with his crowd, the Savage (mine) gang, to have courted praise from a school marm. It was not the lack of opportunity that cut short his education but the fact that the roaring frontier outside the classroom made school the dullest place in town. Both of Johnny's older sisters were often on the school honor rolls published in the Virginia City papers, but a diligent search through many issues of the old files has yet to reveal the name of Johnny Waldorf among the elect.

Yet he read his way up and down the shelves of the Miners' Union Library, from A through Z, from adventure through romance, from philosophy through travels. Those shelves were filled with more than two thousand books continually added to in the years after the Great Fire of October 26, 1875, and the newspapers frequently ran long lists of books donated by interested townsmen or ordered from eastern publishers. It was a wide and wonderful field for a boy who loved the printed word.

The larrupings Jacob Waldorf gave to his eldest son were evidence of a father's concern for the boy. He loved and cherished his family, but tenderness was not part of the nature of a man who daily risked his life in depths that could produce 130 degrees of temperature and were perennially as dark as the regions of hell but for the eerie light of yellow lantern and candle glow.

Johnny revered his father but found him a little like Jehovah, descending from his remote realm to wield the lightning rod of discipline.

Jacob Waldorf worked an eight-hour day, seven days a week around the calendar, whether as a pick-and-shovel miner or a shift boss. All through those hours Jacob and the men with him toiled with the unending terrors of the mine from one thousand to two thousand feet and more below the surface. As Eliot Lord observed, only the hardiest and the most skilled miners remained on the job, partly because of the standards set by the Miners' Union, partly because it took a peculiar and tenacious courage to face that heat and peril day after day.[3]

The miners lived constantly with the danger of fire, of cave-in, of spurting hot water, of insidiously seeping gases, of falling into the scalding sump—of a hundred emergencies that could and did happen. Men who worked even a few minutes beyond their endurance had been known to sit down finally to rest— and to die in an instant. Even when a shift was over, a man risked death rising in the open cage, for a sudden faintness, as it lifted through the dark, could send him slumping against the shaft wall and instant, mangling death, unless his comrades were quick to sense his weakness and grip his sagging body. Death was waiting even at the surface when, after a shift in volcanic heat, they emerged into bitter mountain weather that chilled them with every breath. More than one miner arrived home with walking pneumonia, and many died of it.

In 1880, for instance—when there were fewer miners working, for the long decline had already set in—mining accidents accounted for twenty-eight deaths while pneumonia took thirty-one, the highest figure in a total of 280 deaths for the year.[4]

If a miner took Sunday off to attend church with his family, it was out of his own pocket, out of his four dollars a day as a miner, or five dollars a day as a shift boss. The consequent absence of miners from Sunday services depressed the clergy in town. They thought men who faced such dangers should be allowed a little time for giving thanks to God in church of a Sunday.[5]

Jacob Waldorf was a reverent man but not reverent enough

to dock himself a day's pay four Sundays a month—not with a family that had increased to three boys and four girls by 1881. Respect for the law and reverence for the God of the frontier, however, were qualities Jacob Waldorf insisted on in his children. By practical demonstration of the strap, he convinced them that virtue was by far the safer course of conduct. His ideals, his code, and his insistence on punctuality remained with all of them throughout their lives.

In Johnny's boyhood world it was a matter of etiquette to boast about one's father. By the time he was nine, Johnny's brag took on a swagger. His father began to act and talk like a man getting ready to run for office. The torch that lit the fires of zeal and service to a cause in Jacob Waldorf was the *Virginia Evening Chronicle*, a paper of avowed Democratic persuasion and an outspoken enemy of the Virginia and Truckee Railroad. Jacob Waldorf was a Northern Democrat, a political view carried over from his upstate New York boyhood. He had continued to be a Democrat all during the war that split the party and the nation, and had been a Democrat through ten years passed in a town that was solidly Republican at the polls.

Jacob shared the *Chronicle's* conviction that something should be done about the V. & T. For as the seventies waned and the eighties began, Jacob as well as the entire town began to sense that the Comstock's world was running down. Yet nobody wanted to admit that the big boom was coming to an end. They blamed the high freight rates of the V. & T., which had a monopoly on transporting almost everything, living and inanimate, that moved in and out of Virginia City. Horse-drawn wheels on the Geiger Grade and through Gold Canyon had long since given up the fight, except for an occasional truck rumbling through the old tunnel between Virginia City and Gold Hill.

In their anger with the Virginia and Truckee, the miners and mine owners were as one. All were convinced that if the Nevada legislature would stop being gentle with the railroad and pass a bill forcing freight rates down, business would boom. And if business boomed again, they just might buy time enough for the discovery of the next Big Bonanza—bigger even than the wonder of 1873. It seemed such a simple answer.

The *Chronicle* reporter who inspired Jacob Waldorf and his fellow miners to a crusading spirit was Arthur McEwen, a Scotsman destined to become one of America's more famous and colorful journalists. McEwen, just twenty-eight, already loved an editorial fight for the underdog and was merciless when he went into action. He had come up to the Comstock "from the Bay" in January, 1879, to cover the legislature for Denis McCarthy, owner of the *Chronicle*. McCarthy belonged to a group which thought the legislature was owned by the V. & T. Within a few months, McEwen's coverage of the activities of that legislature made life so unpleasant for a number of its members that they were said to have left Nevada, never to return. McEwen worked for the *Chronicle* for no more than two years, but he made his mark in Virginia City annals.[6]

Although the town's two larger papers, the *Chronicle* and the *Enterprise*, differed sharply in politics and their views of the V. & T., Jacob Waldorf subscribed to both. And when he read them, it was a time of silence throughout the little house, for he had a long arm and a considerable force in its swing when he was displeased with his progeny, especially exuberant Johnny. One of the memories the boy carried with him when he finally left home was that of his father's lean length stretched on the parlor floor at night in front of the tingling potbellied stove, a miner's candle lighting the pages as he made his way slowly, often whispering as if savoring the words, through the day's news, editorials, foreign and national dispatches, local items, and the stock reports. From it all he formed his philosophy and his political convictions.

The legislature of 1879 repeated the disappointments and failures of previous sessions. Legislators who pledged at the time of election to do something about the exorbitant freight rates had, according to the *Chronicle*, sold out again to the "railroad crowd." McEwen, naming names, referred to "male Magdalens" and "slaves of the sack" who had sold their "small souls" in Carson City.[7]

"The majority of both Houses being confessedly Hessians in the employ of the railroads, all efforts to pass bills which would be disagreeable to their masters are quite useless," read his dispatch of March 6, 1879. "It was," he said the next day, "the old story of a few upright men fighting a hopeless fight against an irresistible number of rascals."[8]

Getting the "rascals" out of office became the objective of mass meetings, petitions, and hoarse oratory. One day, in a story about a former legislator's being found unconscious in his cups, McEwen remarked: "He is not the first man who has been ruined by election to office. It is hard to come down to honest labor and $4 a day after a year's ease, high salary and perquisites."[9]

In January 1880, Johnny heard the news that had been brewing for weeks: his father had been elected president of the Miners' Union of Virginia City. It was a position of power but one limited to just six months. No man could succeed himself or serve another term at a later time. Only the offices of treasurer and secretary could ever be held by re-election, and they were reserved for disabled miners.

In October of 1880, after his six months' term had ended, Jacob Waldorf offered himself on the altar of patriotism as a candidate for sheriff of Storey County, "subject to the decision of the Democratic County Convention." Instead, Jacob found himself selected as a candidate for the Nevada assembly.[10]

In 1880, former Union General Winfield Scott Hancock was the Democratic candidate for president of the United States. He was picked as the only candidate who might weld together the northern and chivalry factions of the Democratic party and ease the fears of Republicans, who had long suspected all Democrats of being anything from horse thieves to unreconstructed rebels. It was the first year the Democrats of Storey County saw any chance of having their candidates elected. It also was the first year that Johnny took an interest in politics, later to become the very stuff of his life. He never got over the first excitement of torchlight parades and full-flung oratory, although in 1880 his participation was limited to driving additional nails into his father's new high board fence until they spelled out Hancock.

In spite of Johnny's contribution to the campaign, Hancock lost to James A. Garfield. But Arthur McEwen was awarded an elegant gold watch by the Democrats of Storey County with effusive expressions of gratitude for his editorial genius. The candidates of the Democratic party had swept the county for the first time in Nevada's history.[11]

Jacob Waldorf's campaign also was successful, but not entirely because of McEwen's crusade. He was popular with the miners in spite of his strait-laced views on tobacco and liquor. They called him "Ophir Jake," a nickname he may have earned in 1877, when his faith in Ophir stock lost him a dream fortune, or back in 1871, when he first came to the Comstock and his booming voice was heard shouting from the depths of the Ophir to the man at the top of the shaft. The miners knew Jacob to be a man they could depend upon in an emergency. They accepted his prejudices, respected his integrity, and admired his cussing vocabulary, which spanned a full spectrum of colorful and smouldering comment. Jacob D. Waldorf won a seat in the Nevada assembly with one of the highest pluralities in Storey County.

On January 3, 1881, he appeared at the tall stone capitol in Carson City, ready for business. The *Journal* of the tenth session testifies to his industry, his impatience with superfluous talk, his dedication to the pledges of the campaign to reduce railroad rates. He became a member of the Committee for Military and Indian Affairs and was the assemblyman delegated to nominate bonanza king James G. Fair for United States senator. He was also the author of what Arthur McEwen referred to as "the Waldorf bill," intended to check, curb, and control the Virginia and Truckee Railroad.

Whatever was said about James G. Fair in later years, he was the miners' friend in the election of 1880, the one man they believed could protect their interests in the U.S. Senate. It was an honor to be the man chosen to nominate Fair for such a high office, especially since he would run against William E. Sharon. It was also an honor to be the man to engineer the "radical" railroad bill through the assembly. Johnny must have read the *Virginia Evening Chronicle* with great pride as he followed his father's career in the capitol.

On January 25, 1881, Jacob Waldorf introduced the bill that

would reduce railroad rates and return prosperity to the silver mining towns. Headlines in the *Chronicle* shouted the news:

THE STRUGGLE BEGUN

WALDORF OF STOREY THROWS DOWN THE GAUNTLET

HE INTRODUCES A RADICAL RAILROAD BILL

AN EXAMINATION OF THE BOOKS CALLED FOR[12]

The dispatch that day gave the details: "Mr. Waldorf, having got the floor, asked permission to introduce a bill without previous notice, and nobody having any suspicion of the nature of the measure, no objection was made. The bill was passed to the clerk Lowery, and notwithstanding the phenomenally bad reading of this functionary, the document made a greater stir than anything that has been murdered in the reading since the convening of this body."[13]

The Waldorf bill limited the rate per mile charged for passengers and freight, provided for reduced rates for children under twelve, demanded that there be no discrimination in accepting freight or passengers, and called for a fine of $2,000 for any violations of the provisions of the bill—with an additional $500 reward to the informer of any violations.

"During the reading of the bill (and it was so read that the author was forced to squirm in his chair)," reported McEwen, "there was a deep silence and fixity of attention that has not hitherto been paid to any piece of manuscript that has fallen into the hands of the clerk. When the misery was over and Mr. Lowery had resumed his seat and the stroking of his moustache, Waldorf controlled his feelings and rose to his feet. He moved that the bill be referred to the Committee on Railroads and Corporations."

The assembly chamber resounded with the uproar. But Jacob held the floor and presented a resolution instructing the committee to inquire into the subject of freight and passenger rates on railroads "the termini of which is within the state." This was aimed straight at the Virginia and Truckee.

To protests that such inspection of the records would interfere with the railroad's bookkeeping, Jacob replied that he "hadn't lost any railroads and was in favor of getting down to business and fulfilling the pledges of the delegation.

On February 1, McEwen reported that the chairman of the assembly Committee on Railroads and Corporations had asked him to notify all persons "having complaint to make against the railroad company to send such complaints to the committee or to appear in person" at the meeting the following day.[14] McEwen was dubious and commented that "if the people who suffer from the railroads haven't the pluck to make their grievances known, they don't deserve sympathy if they don't get relief."

Apparently, no one showed up at the meeting or made a written complaint. The majority report presented to the assembly was a whitewash of the railroad's tactics. Only one member dissented. He was John Smyth of Austin, Lander County. But one vote wasn't going to be of much help to Jacob Waldorf. "It long since became evident that this legislature will do nothing disagreeable to the railroads," growled McEwen. "The furore of two years ago having apparently died out completely, there is no particular reason why anybody else should waste his strength in useless indignation."[15]

But Jacob Waldorf refused to give up so quickly. He knew the pressures that could be put on people about to testify against the power of the railroad. Hopeless or not, he was going to make a fight for his bill. He did it with all the flourishes and fervor of traditional frontier oratory. But McEwen refused to appreciate the zeal of Jacob Waldorf.

"Waldorf made a glowing speech in favor of his bill," he wrote. "It was probably the finest oratorical effort ever essayed in the Assembly Chamber. . . . Mr. Waldorf's argument was perhaps somewhat obscured by the ornate style of his delivery. But what are facts compared with the flowers of rhetoric? He asked everbody to stand shoulder to shoulder with him and move in solid phalanx up against the Monster Monopoly which was sitting down upon the respiratory organs of the body politic. He closed by making the timely inquiry, 'Do the railroads own the people or do the people own the railroads?' As Mr. Waldorf closed he was rewarded by a burst of applause."[16]

One of Jacob's colleagues arose when the applause had sub-

From the upright union of the stern, God-fearing miner "Ophir Jake" Waldorf and his wife Adeline (above)—a teacher who endured their Comstock days as "temporary"—sprang pixie Johnny (right). Arriving in Virginia City in high-button shoes at age three, he spent thirteen spirited years there.

While a cub reporter, Waldorf married a little auburn-haired New England nurse named Daisy Garnett. Dolores, their first-born, arrived in 1896. Despite manifold adventures in his long career as a newspaperman, Waldorf (shown at the right in his later years) enshrined the Comstock as an island of sunlight, affection, and excitement, shining at the very center of his memories.

sided and moved that the bill be "indefinitely postponed." After all, the majority report could find "nothing to find fault with in the management and charges of the railroad."

His defense of the railroad bill was Jacob's first and last attempt at oratory. It got him only Arthur McEwen's sarcasm and the faithless defection of fellow assemblymen. It would be many years before a railroad bill was passed. Humiliated, disgusted with politics, and smarting from the sting of McEwen's veiled ridicule, Jacob Waldorf went back into the mine. He refused ever to enter politics again. "I can't go that railroad crowd," was his only comment.

Johnny always spoke of his father's brief career in the assembly with a touch of sad concern, a tone of wistfulness. During the months the boy followed McEwens' exciting accounts and the grim stories of what the crusade had come to, he developed a cynicism he would never lose. Like many sons of reformers, he saw how often stalemate, frustration, ridicule, and bitterness seemed to be the only rewards for faith, courage, and dedication. But McEwen had revealed to the boy the charms and excitement, the color and variety of journalism. Twenty-four years later, the miner's son and McEwen, on one of his periodical breaks with William Randolph Hearst and the New York *American*, would find themselves fellow members of Fremont Older's *Bulletin* staff crusading against Eugene Schmitz and Abraham Ruef.

The years following Jacob Waldorf's defeat at the legislature were not happy ones. Little Gertrude, born in late 1881, died in April 1882. To a family already plagued with troubles, the death of the baby was a shock that marked them all with a poignant, never quite conquered sense of loss. She was the seventh child and—like Wordsworth's mourners—the family remained always seven in their hearts. Grandchildren who never saw the little grave in Virginia City's Masonic cemetery felt the tragedy of her death in a wistful story told many times.

Heartbroken Addie, always willing to believe the prophecies of tea leaves, the feathering lines in the palm of a hand, or the portents of apple peelings tossed over a shoulder, consulted Mrs. Sandy Bowers, the Washoe seeress, many times in hopes of receiving some message from her vanished baby. Mrs. Bowers was not taken lightly by Addie or the mining community, which consulted her regarding the whereabouts of rich veins of ore, the future of stocks, the fate of lost watches and missing men.

As time went on, Johnny began to dream of the ocean. It seemed to offer more than the scene that stretched endlessly east of Sugar Loaf, a landscape of mountains and desert and dusty infinity. To stay in Virginia City meant becoming an engine wiper in the mines, an apprentice for the darkness below. The little house was becoming very crowded. There were quarrels with his younger brother George, who probably infringed on jealously guarded property rights. More than once Johnny tried to run away, furious with an indignation that soon passed.

When he did go down over the Geiger Grade at sixteen, the curly-headed rebel could not help but expect the world to be as friendly as Virginia City had been. He could imagine no other world, but he was no tenderfoot. More than twelve years in a mining camp had conditioned him to the violence of direct action, both at home and with the gang. His father had great faith in a "good belt" taking care of many an upstart evil. Bad table manners put more than one ravenous Waldorf boy on the floor with a powerful backhand swing of Dad's reproving arm. As a father, Jacob Waldorf left nothing to be desired in the way of good nourishing food, warm clothing, and home remedies. His house was weathertight, his woodshed well supplied; he paid his bills on pay day and often boasted that he had the handsomest privy on the hill, but it would be years before the boy fully understood the man.

Along with the memories of his rough rearing, Johnny took with him a better legacy. Throughout his life, pioneer ideals of cautious thrift mingled with the reckless hopes of a miner expecting a bonanza and with the love of melodrama, sentimental ballads, black-faced minstrels, dirty-faced boys, and an impulsive pity for blind beggars—the heritage of terror in a mine tunnel when the light went out. He could never pass a blind beggar without dropping a half dollar in the cup. He was the easiest touch from coast to coast and the quickest to forget.

By the time he became an apprentice printer in San Jose,

California, he had learned that the world has many moods and many faces, most of them harsh and cold. He had learned that a kid with only a grammar school education is no hero out of a book rocketing to quick riches. He had many adventures as errand boy and bellhop, wandering to nameless places, learning to ride the rods of a freight train, balancing on the roofs of box cars, swinging aboard empties when they were safely away from towns. He had walked ties for miles, camped by the right of way, once ran for his life ahead of a wall of flame as a forest fire started by some tramp's forgotten fire roared hot and hungry behind him. His travels as a tramp printer carried him to the Atlantic, along the eastern seaboard through a total of forty-six states. Always a man for statistics, he could name them in a chant many years later.

In 1893 Johnny returned from the Chicago World's Fair to enter the composing room of the San Jose *Mercury*, hold every office but sergeant-at-arms in the local chapter of the International Typographical Union, and serve a term as president of the Federated Trades Council of Santa Clara County. He carried a little brass printer's rule in his vest pocket to the day of his death, but in 1895 he left the composing room to become a reporter for the *Mercury*.

He had confided his dreams of becoming a writer to a little auburn-haired New Englander, Daisy E. Garnett, and she had not laughed. She was a registered nurse and doctor's assistant in San Jose preparing for advanced studies at New York's Bellevue Hospital, but she was sure that Jack, as he was often called, would go far with encouragement. Bellevue faded from her future. She called him Laddie and he called her Midget. They were married on October 17, 1895.

Ten years later, if Jack Waldorf had taken the time, he could have looked back on enough excitement and variety to put even fabulous Virginia City in the shade. In 1896 he was the first reporter on the scene of the Dunham murders amidst the flowering orchards of the Santa Clara Valley. The story was a classic in western journalism, as bizarre and gory as an Indian massacre. One man had killed six people near Campbell Station in a night of apparently premeditated violence. In the blue light before dawn on May 27, 1896, the sheriff, a deputy, and Jack Waldorf found people they all knew well lying sprawled in death about the barnyard and the silent house. The last body found—and probably the first killed—was that of twenty-six-year-old Hattie Dunham, whose neck was broken. Her three-week-old son lay in the bed beside her, snuffling and hungrily turning his head from side to side. He had not been touched. Jim Dunham, Hattie's husband had vanished and was never found.[17]

Later that year began months of work poring through once-scorned school books, preparing for entrance examinations to Stanford University, which he passed nicely.

Jack Waldorf's brief college career began in 1897 and ended in 1898. To cover expenses, Jack pedaled his bicycle like a racer about Palo Alto and the Stanford campus, gathering items which he sent off to the San Jose *Mercury* and the San Francisco *Chronicle*. Home was a little cottage far east of the railroad tracks. Midget used to say they lived on beans and skimmed milk.

By late August 1898, he was working in San Francisco, searching out clues in the Botkin case for the *Chronicle* and writing stories on space rates. Already the father of a daughter, he had acquired a son on the girl's second birthday, and college had to be put aside "for awhile."

The Botkin murders were in their way as bizarre as the Dunham murders. They had taken place in Dover, Delaware. Both of the victims, Mrs. John Dunning and Mrs. John P. Deane, were daughters of a former member of Congress. Poisoned candy had been mailed to Mrs. Dunning from San Francisco. Eventually Mrs. Cordelia Botkin was discovered to have been the donor of the anonymous and lethal gift. Mrs. Botkin, it seems, was a jealous woman. John Dunning, a wire service manager in San Francisco, had been her lover until Mrs. Dunning packed and went home to father. Dunning then decided to end the affair in order to woo his wife back again. Mrs. Botkin was not pleased.[18]

At the end of his first week with the San Francisco *Chronicle*, Jack Waldorf had pasted up enough copy to pay him about seventy dollars at space rates. His delight at the prospect of all that money evaporated when he learned that he had instead been put on a weekly salary—at no more than a third of that figure. But weekly pay checks meant a steady job, something he needed now that he was father of two children. He tossed the pasted-up copy away.

The change in finances recalled an experience during his bicycle delivery days for a San Francisco bakery in 1886, shortly after he had run away from Virginia City. He had been given a container of charlotte russe to deliver to the de Young family. It was a special rush order. A rumbling dray drawn by heavy-footed horses all but side-swiped his bicycle as he was pedaling at top speed. The cover jiggled loose from the container and a fine gray dust settled on the pristine charlotte russe. Johnny may not have known that the de Young family owned the San Francisco *Chronicle*, but he did know that they were important enough to have him fired if they complained about the condition of the charlotte russe. So he took a pencil from back of his ear and stirred the charlotte russe very carefully. When it appeared once more clean and white, he made the delivery.

"And that," Jack used to conclude with a chuckle, "was when *I* made Mike de Young eat dirt!"

After several years of covering police and city hall beats for the *Chronicle*—long periods of waiting and card-playing broken by explosions of tension and confusion—Jack Waldorf became John Taylor Waldorf and joined the staff of Fremont Older, managing editor of the San Francisco *Bulletin*. Already, Older had made a devastating crusader of the paper and was picking his staff carefully.

The transfer of allegiance to the *Bulletin* was accompanied by the shaving of his Stevensonian mustache, to the consternation of his three terrified children when he came home after the transformation. He began wearing black, wide-brimmed Stetson hats and elastic, pull-on gaiters—items that became his hallmark for the rest of his life. Both were reminiscent of Virginia City, of men an admiring boy had watched on the planked sidewalks of C Street, telling stories and stamping their feet.

Those were the days of violent strife within the city of San

Francisco. Older was suspicious of Eugene Schmitz, San Francisco's handsome mayor, and of Abe Ruef, the wily political boss who pulled the strings that activated both the mayor and the Board of Supervisors. Many assignments were turned over to John Waldorf. He became a man to send on special stories, —to Oregon on a land fraud case involving a U.S. senator, or down to Los Angeles to review the production of a traveling theatrical troupe before it came north (Older was having a bitter quarrel with local theater managers).

In spite of his tailoring, a fondness for classical literature, and considerable sophistication, the kid from the Comstock remained in command of the man. His shock of lazy brown curls tumbled down his forehead as of old, no matter how short he had the barber cut them or how often he nervously combed them into order. His black felt hat had an angle for every mood. In competition it tilted belligerently down over his eyes; in friendly conversation it leaned rakishly right or left; and when a door slammed shut and a story seemed blocked, it shot back in consternation.

A realist by nature and experience, John Waldorf was in his element in newspaper work, but he had no illusions about it. One day his little daughter came home from second grade in tearful fury. A schoolmate had said his father was a better man than hers.

"What does his father do?" asked John Waldorf.

"He collects garbage!" sobbed the little girl.

"The kid may be right!" hooted her father, shaking with laughter.

Waldorf's stories had taken on a rural flavor after his family moved to farms, first at Petaluma in the Sonoma County poultry belt, then at Beresford and Belmont down the Peninsula, and finally at Cupertino. He may have exaggerated the number of cows he milked, if any, or the number of feathers his eggless hens shed, or the extent of feather blooms which were the only things harvested from his strawberry patch; but they made good telling. Midget's troubles with a hysterical black horse named Bess, who resented the arrival of the gas engine and made every journey to the Beresford and Belmont railroad stations to meet the commuter an adventure of great drama, were told at many a dinner table.

But there was always the charm of Virginia City shining in the background, recalled in stories told to his eager children. Those stories took on a promise of wider interest when in the fall of 1904 Fremont Older added a Sunday feature to the *Bulletin*, a staff writers' section. In it appeared articles, essays, verse, fiction, satire, serials, and interviews. Two young cartoonists, Rube Goldberg and Herb Roth, were among the illustrators assigned to the new Sunday section. Herb Roth, who drew the blithe illustrations for John Waldorf's reminiscences, dreamed of moving over into fine arts and was saving money to study in Europe. It was an ambition eventually realized, but when he returned to the United States, it was to work on papers in New York.

The great Arthur McEwen, displeased with some policy of William Randolph Hearst's, had quit the New York *American* in 1905 and come west to help Older in his crusade to eliminate Eugene Schmitz and Abraham Ruef from the civic scene. He wrote full-page spreads for the special section, articles as abrasive as any Johnny had read in the old *Virginia Evening Chronicle* so long before.

There were whimsical essays by Edward F. O'Day, stories by Lowell Otis Reese and Waldemar Young, and Pauline Jacobson's famous interviews, written with weary reluctance, infallible skill, and complete disregard for deadlines. There was a great variety of copy by John Taylor Waldorf: essays, fiction based on his tramp printer experiences, satires in offerings patterned after Pepys, and finally in March 1905, the first of the reminiscences of the days when he was a kid on the Comstock.

The recollections of his boyhood did not run consecutively. They were often interrupted by other material, chiefly fiction, taken apparently from standby "holdover" while he was on special assignment elsewhere. One interruption came in mid-September of 1905 when he took Midget over the Sierra and through Gold Canyon to visit the scenes of that wonderful boyhood.

It was not long after his return to San Francisco that a lullaby he had written was set to music. While it may not have been inspired wholly by the return to Virginia City, it recalls a vivid memory of his mother in inconsolable grief after the death of little Gertrude. The lullaby converts the baby girl to a boy, but the mother rocks in anguish just as his mother had. Entitled "Singing an Angel to Sleep," it was set to music by Wilton Thompson. It was just the sort of lugubrious song popular in the Civil War days, dripping with implications of a high mortality rate, sadly sentimental, the kind of song that would have been a smash hit in the Virginia City of the seventies, when miners toughened by constant danger had to be hit over the head with sodden tenderness before emotion overcame them.

This mining camp need of impact stayed with John Waldorf all his life, whether it was drama, opera, fiction, popular music, speeches, or political candidates. "It's got to hit me here," he used to say, thumping a clenched fist against his breast. The same need was apparent when in the spring of 1916 he was among those attending a White House reception for members of Congress and their staffs. His face was drawn in apprehension as he came out of the long receiving line. Woodrow Wilson's handshake had lacked the grip, the crushing pressure of a Colonel Fair campaigning along C Street! Just how the scholarly Wilson could have crushed hands in a line two thousand handshakes long was not the question. Wilson simply lacked impact.

Another poignant moment from the past took life again in November 1905, when Fremont Older and the *Bulletin* lost the fight to beat the Schmitz-Ruef ticket in San Francisco on election day. Arthur McEwen's articles about what he often described as "the plunder-bund" had not convinced San Francisco voters of the need for reform, nor had Older's well-planned crusade.

The opposition to Schmitz was crushed by a huge vote which sent him and his crew back to City Hall for a third round. It was a cruel blow indeed to Older, who was positive that the Schmitz-Ruef combine was sacking the town. Besides, he was trying to save a tired old paper from severe circulation problems which the loss of the campaign would only aggravate.

Older was in shock after the defeat, but McEwen fairly

breathed smoke and fire when the election was over. Sitting in the dim *Bulletin* office surrounded by discarded tally sheets after the returns were in, John Waldorf could see how Arthur McEwen reacted to defeat. The Comstock miner's son saw the same fury that McEwen had displayed as a young man when the Waldorf bill was defeated at Carson City. He raged against the gullible public whom he both defended and despised. At that very moment that public was celebrating riotously in the streets outside the *Bulletin*, while the men who had tried to protect them sat alone in misery. The screams, the shouts, the whoosh of rockets, the hoots and smashing of glass as rocks were heaved through the *Bulletin* windows—all of it came up to the men holding the wake in the city room.

Older later recalled in *My Own Story* how they sat silent in despair while McEwen raved about the rotten town and said he was going back to New York the next day.[19] He did and was welcomed into the fold by a forgiving William Randolph Hearst, whose San Francisco *Examiner* had not agreed with the *Bulletin's* headlined suspicions during the 1905 campaign.

When Older recovered from the shock of the loss, he put the staff to hunting evidence of corruption at City Hall. John Waldorf was one of the men who watched every move of the Schmitz administration, high and low. Week by week, the hunches were followed to facts, the immunity of obvious houses of prostitution investigated, and the implications of shady deals studied—deals ranging from prize fight permits to railroad franchises.

In the early weeks of 1906, a series of fiction stories by John Taylor Waldorf began to appear in the special writer's section. "The Jumping Off Place" was the title of the third installment which appeared on Sunday, April 15, 1906. It was to be continued, but three days later the paper, the town, the hopeful copy—all—became ashes. What John Waldorf always reverently described as "the biggest story of them all," the earthquake and fire of April 18, 1906, interrupted a great many things, including the never-completed serial.

When publication of the *Bulletin* was resumed on April 21, it appeared through the courtesy of the Oakland *Herald*. San Francisco was a mass of rubble and smoking ruins, and John

Taylor Waldorf responded to a wire from the Oregon *Journal*. He was wanted as city editor. Less than a year later, he was back at the "damned old ash pile," a fountain pen bound with engraved sterling silver in his pocket, a gift of the *Journal* staff. Midget would have liked to stay on in Portland, but John had received an offer from the *Morning Call* in San Francisco. The graft prosecution was at hand. It was too good a story to miss.

It wasn't long before he was back again with Older as the drama of the *Bulletin's* part in the graft prosecution unfolded. To Older everyone investigated by the graft prosecution, especially Abe Ruef, was a devil with horns, hooves, and tail. He was utterly unable to understand how anyone could see human decency in such black-hearted evildoers. But Ruef had a great deal of wit and charm, and few newspapermen, John Waldorf among them, could hate him as Older hated him in the beginning.

There is a story that the famous sportswriter, W. O. (Bill) McGeehan, a genial, soft-spoken man who liked everyone most of the time, met Ruef during an interlude in the trials when McGeehan was still a cityside reporter. They had a drink together. When Older learned of this sociability, he went into a shouting fury. McGeehan always declared, according to Evelyn Wells in her biography of Fremont Older, that Older's hair began to turn from black to gray during that one terrible tirade.[20]

This experience of Bill McGeehan's no doubt gave caution to any display of friendship for Ruef by John Taylor Waldorf. In later years, however, he often told of an occasion when Ruef was on the stand during the trials and Waldorf, covering for the *Bulletin*, was tilted back in his chair at the press table, balancing it on two legs with a skill developed during long years of practice. This time balance and skill failed him. The chair fell with a rending and splintering of wood as 200 pounds of Fourth Estate crashed to the floor.

Abe Ruef turned a quick and bland smile on the judge as the red-faced reporter struggled to rise. "You see, your Honor," beamed Ruef, "my testimony has floored the *Bulletin!*"

With the success of the graft prosecution—which ultimately

jailed Schmitz and Ruef, but none of the "higherups," as Older used to describe them—the *Bulletin* was off to a career of crusades. With every one, the paper discovered more and more evil to denounce.

John Taylor Waldorf, who became Older's editorial writer, complete with all three names for a byline, was as devoted to the right as either Fremont Older or Arthur McEwen, if a little more contained. But he was beginning to be a bit cynical about a starry-eyed zeal that pursued one crusade after another, exposing wickedness from the Bay to the sea. Like his father, Older and McEwen could not change the world of men and lost more often than they won. Perhaps the fact that the three men had a vague physical resemblance to one another—tall, lean-faced with high foreheads and deepset eyes—and shared a perennial, unswerving dedication to the causes they supported, gave strength to his cynicism. They were at heart frontier evangelists, men of another day.

When Older decided upon the crusade to abolish betting on horse races, he struck close to the heart of his editorial writer. Betting on the horses was to John Waldorf what speculating in mining stock had been to his father—and he lost just about as often. But Older was positive that betting shattered homes, impoverished families, spread evil through every racetrack community. He may have been quite right, but John Waldorf had some unhappy reservations.

He liked horse racing so well that he kept a little notebook in a vest pocket in which he wrote the names of horses that occurred to him during conversation or on the long commuter rides to and from San Francisco. The name might be suggested by the title of a book or a song or mention of a friend's name. It would bring a sudden glint to his eyes as he exclaimed, "That's the name of a race horse!" Out would come the little black book and down would go the name for future reference when he made out his dope sheet. His was a peculiar system for playing the races, two-thirds hunch, the rest faith in the law of averages. His selections seldom won. In fact, his only big killing at the track came at Saratoga, New York, years later.

John Taylor Waldorf's editorials on the evils of playing the races scorched the pastime with a fiery and pious denunciation that he did not feel and that he achieved solely in the line of duty. The more he denounced horse-race gambling, the more there grew a nagging doubt as to his own journalistic integrity.

Older and his editorial writer had a great deal to do with killing horse racing in California, for without betting it lost appeal for many years. But it was done at a great cost to the peace of mind of a man whose heart bled with every word. He used to say that he steeled himself for each day's scathing editorial with a pint of fortitude from the Golden Rule downstairs, and the flask stood before him on the desk to bolster his flagging spirits as he wrote. When the fluid in the flask was down and the editorial was complete, there remained but one solace: "I'd turn the copy over to Older, grab my hat, and run like hell to catch the ferry in time for the last race at Emeryville!"

A bitter note edged his laughter. He began wryly to describe himself as a "journalistic street walker"[21] to look with sour skepticism on the do-gooder and the zealot. Ardent young reporters, just out of college and proud to worship at Fremont Older's feet, thought Waldorf amusing but eccentric.

Perhaps his father's death in 1910 had something to do with his sharpening point of view. It revived memories of a lone man fighting for what he believed to be right, preferring to go down in the mine and face death every day rather than compromise his convictions. John Taylor Waldorf apparently wondered if he might be in danger of compromising his convictions, even if Older's crusades were all against those who prey on frailty.

Jacob Waldorf had in fact been poignantly consistent in death at seventy. Straight and stern, with a long white beard, living on a Civil War pension for which he had reluctantly applied long after he quit Virginia City, he was just as stalwart, just as intelligent as ever. But who wanted a man of seventy for any job? He longed to prove his worth.

One morning his son George, an attorney, gave Jacob a sheaf of clients' bills to collect. Jacob's instructions were to take his time—there was no rush. But by noon of that warm April day in San Jose, he was hurrying back to his son's office, all the bills collected. Jacob had proved he could do as well or better than a young fellow, but it was a victory which death blighted in stride. He was dead as he fell.

Two years later, the miner's other son came to a sharp corner in his career. It was the summer of 1912 and Theodore Roosevelt had made the presidential campaign a three-cornered fight, with William Howard Taft and Woodrow Wilson in the other corners. Older decided to support Roosevelt, whom he knew and admired. It would be up to John Taylor Waldorf to write the *Bulletin* editorials in support of Teddy.

When Older told him, Waldorf was aghast. He refused to have anything to do with it. They had disagreed before but this was a bitter quarrel. Waldorf, who loved drama, appeals to emotion, and crescendo climaxes—back of the footlights—disliked Theodore Roosevelt for his drama, including San Juan Hill, Panama, the Big Stick, and bolting the Republican party. He had read Woodrow Wilson's speeches, followed his brief career in New Jersey politics, and admired his policies. Whether in his mood of rebellion he could have composed editorials supporting William Howard Taft no one would ever know.

When the sounds of violent argument in Older's office subsided, Waldorf chose stubbornly to take a place at the *Bulletin's* copy desk, where he edited stories and counted heads, to the amazement of the young reporters, including Robert L. Duffus, who recalled the scene many years later when he had long been chief editorial writer of the New York *Times*.[22] The young reporters began to think that Waldorf meant what he said about journalistic streetwalkers.

The rift with Older widened. Waldorf remained adamant. He finally left the paper to join the publicity staff for the Panama Pacific International Exposition, taking shape out at the Marina. Later, he directed publicity for the senatorial campaign of James D. Phelan, who twice had been mayor of San Francisco before Eugene Schmitz took office.

Extremely wealthy, Phelan was a new sort of millionaire to the man from Virginia City, very different from the flamboyant silver kings. The only son of a gold rush banker, Phelan was a scholarly, idealistic poet of a man, with a professor's beard. Aloof and introverted, he always impressed his breezy, gregarious publicity man as being a little afraid of friendship, as if he feared that people were warm and familiar because of his money, never himself.

Phelan won, and when John Taylor Waldorf was called to Washington, D.C., he was like a man heading for Mecca. He had been appointed enrolling and engrossing clerk of the U.S. Senate, a post empty since the death of a man who had held it for some thirty years. Although he received the appointment on Phelan's patronage, he was told the job could be his for as long as he wanted, politics being less important than copy-desk skills and editorial experience.

It opened a new world to the ex-newspaperman, for it turned out that he had wanted to work in Washington almost as much as he had once wanted to find the ocean. Both disappointed him. It was not many months before he was referring to the Senate as the "Cave of the Winds" and enjoying the somewhat derisive names that men in the secretary of the Senate's office used in referring to the august dignitaries orating beyond the swinging doors across the hall.

It was in Washington that John Waldorf finally came to realize he would never be able to enter politics as a candidate for office. He spoke of it wistfully and often. Every time he walked down the long hall from the Senate to the House of Representatives with a Senate bill in his hand, he realized it all over again. Custom required that the enrolling and engrossing clerk present bills passed by the Senate to the Speaker of the House in person. And it required making something like a speech, however small, in the House of Representatives.

Preparations for those ordeals in Washington were always accompanied by a morning flurry of ripping stiff white collars as he searched for one that wouldn't scratch his neck. When three or four mangled collars lay on the bedroom floor, there would follow the matter of the reluctant collar button, a tussle that verged on fury. When he was finally ready for the drive to the Capitol, he went off as if to a firing squad.

At the doors to the House floor, he was met by the sergeant-at-arms, with whom, after a whispered conference, he walked down the center aisle toward the rostrum. When his companion was recognized, he shouted, "Mr. Speaker, Mr. Waldorf with a message from the Senate."

Immediately there came a sudden thickness in John Waldorf's voice, a flurry of nervous throat clearances, finally the words of the message: simply the number, title, and a brief summary of the bill's contents. Once he had handed it over, he returned to the Senate offices to unwind, his unhappy task of public speaking over until another bill was passed. He was never able to overcome this misery during the entire four years. If he ever wondered if McEwen's scathing account of his father's oratory back in 1881 had any effect on these deep inhibitions, he never said. He simply gave up all thought of running for office and confined his speech-making to ghosting speeches for many men, from politicians to captains of industry.

There was very little excitement for an old newspaperman in that government job, except when World War I was declared. He worked all that night, checking, double-checking, copy-reading, proofreading, and haunting the government printing office so that the engrossed declaration would be on Woodrow Wilson's desk by morning. It wasn't that he was especially anxious to hurry up a war in which both his sons would enlist; it was merely the same drive for excellence that had given such pride to his father's brief term in politics and his long career as a Comstock miner. Usually, it took three days to process a bill and send it to the president.

It soon became apparent that John Waldorf was envious of his friends in the Senate press gallery. He was more than a little homesick for the noise and rush of a newspaper office. Not long after the war ended, he went to the New York *Tribune*, where he analyzed and edited Washington news. In a few months he was talking of finding time to write the short stories he had always promised himself he would write—someday. The little notebooks where he stored ideas and titles were dog-eared, thumbed, and so smudged in places that they were almost illegible. He was just fifty, but he spoke seriously of retiring to the country.

It wasn't long before he was back in California, living on a forty-six-acre mountain retreat of redwoods, brooks, ferns, tiger lilies, and manzanita just west of Ukiah in Mendocino County. The house stood at the bottom of a deep canyon, both sides of which were part of the "ranch." Midget used to say they were the only people in California whose property was hung up in front of them like a map on the wall.

There was a barely city-size block of level land, but there was a brook with cascades and tinkling falls that joined a rushing stream called the Orr at the bottom of the canyon. During the rainy months, the creek sounded like the lightning express of the Virginia and Truckee. The deer came down daily to nibble the buds off the fruit trees, the wildcats eyed the chickens, and the coyotes yapped in nervous bursts all night. John Waldorf wrote every day, almost all day. Before long, they were back to beans, and now the milk came out of cans.

Either money ran out completely or a year was not long enough to shake the inhibitions of twenty-five years of writing stories for newspaper readers who wanted no frills. The literal statistics of other people's lives had smothered his muse. Most of all, he could not erase that distrust of rhetoric, flowery or otherwise, that Arthur McEwen had found so annoying years before in Carson City. The stories for which he had selected such euphonious titles did not live as they had lived in his thoughts. Soon the country place was locked but for long weekends and summer vacations.

Instead of returning to newspaper work, he sought the high salaries of the publicity trade. He may have decided that retirement and time to write would require a long-range plan of financing. He became the publicity writer and public relations man for a private utility company, visiting newspapers around the state in the company's campaign against a referendum that would have turned California's water and power over to public ownership. Neither social consciousness nor fears of being a journalistic streetwalker were ever expressed. He was paid to stem the tides of "socialism," and he did.

When that fight was won, the utility company asked him to start a monthly magazine designed to create a new and kindlier image. The referendum had sobered the company, and like the famous Southern Pacific, which some years before had come to a realization of the advantages of being "friendly," the Pacific Gas and Electric Company concluded that now was the time not only to win friends but to influence enemies by a running record of its own good deeds. The magazine was called *The Progress* and is still being published.

But there were no crises in that corporation office, so spacious, immaculate, sterile—and lonely—that could possibly disturb an oldtime reporter and campaigner. Once the magazine had been put to bed each month, he was free to travel, interviewing company oldtimers, gathering material for future articles.

Occasionally, he interrupted those travels about California to detour over to Virginia City. It was thirty-eight years since he had gone down the Geiger Grade to find the ocean and make a fortune. Each time he returned, his welcome from old friends was as warm as ever. Each time, it was as if he were entering his own house after a walk to the store.

He took up Spanish, learning it so quickly and with such fluency that he was soon translating old Spanish folk tales into musical and colloquial English. Still, time hung on his hands. He was bored. Yet he refused to write special articles or take outside publicity jobs offered him by people who wanted his skill and experience.

"When I was young and poorly paid and had a family, I would have jumped at these jobs," he once told a member of his family. "I don't need them now. I pass them on to the young fellows who can use the money as I once could. It all comes too late."

Without worries of any kind, with little or no pressure or so it would seem, John Waldorf's health broke in 1928. Old newspaper comrades said it was the slowed tempo of life that did it. He became familiar with doctors for the first time in his life, and he was a difficult patient. Back on the Comstock, you were dosed with sulphur and molasses, herb brews, lard and axle grease salves, and somehow you got well. Always a self-doser, he expected any medicine to do its work in something under twenty minutes.

There were medical warnings, consultations. It was time to slow down, he was told, time to relax. He could not see how a man could slow down more than he had, and he could not relax. When his family tried to shape his life more nearly to the design of the doctors, he said sourly, "You'd burn my soul to save my body!" When a doctor looked up from the charts to tell him that he had a life expectancy of thirteen years, he said with a teasing smile "Which I won't get. Lay you two to one I won't get it."

Before very long he had vanished from the scenes of pre-scribed rest and relaxation and was headed east, away from medical restrictions. He went to work on the New York *Journal*, where he remained until the summer of 1932 and a vacation in California.

By that time, the Great Depression was in its depths. Con-fusion and despair plagued many a newspaper reporter, young as well as old. Although his job on the *Journal* awaited John Waldorf's return, he decided to pass it up when his vacation came to an end. He told a member of his family that he was going to wire the chance at his job to a young reporter out of work in New York.

"I'll tell him to be at the Desk at the time my wire of resigna-tion should arrive. I think he'll get the job." And so John Wal-dorf signed an end to a newspaper career begun more than thirty-six years before.

Everything went according to plan. The young reporter got the job. When he read of John Waldorf's death the following October, he wrote of what that rescuing wire had meant to him in his letter of sympathy to Midget.

Death was very kind to Johnny Waldorf, the Comstock miner's son. It came gently on a Sunday afternoon as he sat in his big easy chair.

"What time is it?" he asked Midget over his shoulder as he shook out the paper. Before she could answer, time meant nothing at all.

DOLORES BRYANT WALDORF

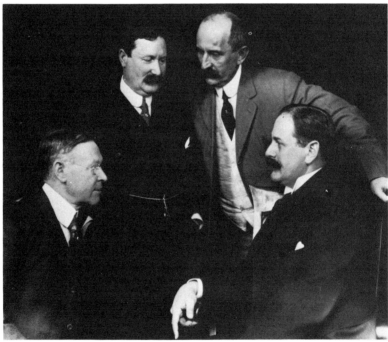

Crusading under the banner headlines of the *Bulletin*, Waldorf took on the dark forces of municipal corruption. Black-hatted political boss Abe Ruef (above), despite whispered help from his attorney, eventually toppled under the forces of civic light manifested by Heney, Burns, Older, and Spreckels, seen below in congenial conference.

San Francisco, the city of style, mood, and corruption. The Spreckles Building (center) dominated the scene, as Spreckles dominated the city's reform movement.

ut to clean up San Francisco,
igar-smoking *Bulletin* editor
remont C. Older (right) was,
t heart, a frontier evangelist.
ight was on his side; so was
x-mayor James D. Phelan (far
ft). Calling the tune for
usician-turned-mayor Eugene
. Schmitz, Ruef (immediate
ft) represented Evil unrepen-
nt. At stake: the cool, gray
ity of love, seen below in a 1910
anorama from the Bay.

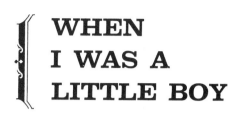

# WHEN
# I WAS A
# LITTLE BOY

N OT LONG AGO I read a book in which a man with a talent for writing simple English told the story of his boyhood. It was not a succession of thrilling adventures. Nothing startling happened at any stage of the narrative, but there was a nameless charm to it that made me think that if all biography were confined to the days of childhood, we should be saved the dusting of an endless number of dull books, to say nothing of the gain in volumes, the reading of which would be worthwhile, if only for the joy that it kindled in the heart.

Our children strike the right note when they plead, "Papa, tell us what you did when you were a little boy." I believe in granting this request, with due reservations, of course. Encouragement of this curiosity may in time bring about a boom in the biography of childhood. The idea grows upon me as I think about it. Perhaps I had better tell something about my own earlier years in order that you, my reader, may get an inkling of the scheme at its worst.

To begin, I was born in a log cabin. Abraham Lincoln was similarly favored, but this merely goes to show that there is a great difference in log cabins. To the best of my recollection, my first three years of life were a blank. At the end of that hiatus, I am told, I distinguished myself by creeping under a gate and joining a crowd that was hurrying downtown to view the remains of a wrecked Fourth of July cannon.

Two things made this escapade notable. The aperture under

the gate, according to authority that I must respect, was so small that the family cat hesitated to use it. The other cause of my early fame was that my relatives took it for granted that one can fly to pieces twice in a day and that I was in grave danger as I stood with critical eye inspecting the fragments of iron and wondering, "was the man hurted much?" I have been told that the man was given a military funeral. He gave his life to his country, my uncle said, but still I was the greater hero.

I couldn't have been much more than three years old when my mother took me down to the river to see some people baptized. My conduct on that occasion was unexpected. To me it appeared that the man who first waded into the river was trying to drown the poor people who followed him in. I screamed in my fright and set up a terrible hullabaloo, but the ceremony went on despite my protest and was, no doubt, a great success. However, that was the last time anyone ever took me to see people baptized.

The two wonderful things just related occurred in Michigan. Long before I reached the age of four, my parents, without waiting for the consent of the governed, decided that I should be moved to Nevada. Father had gone on ahead [May 1871] and the rest of us, four in all [Adeline (Slayton) Waldorf, 33; Minnie Alice, 8; Oriana, 5; Johnny, 3] started westward in a bunch. All I can remember of the journey is that the boys who bathed in the Missouri River beneath the bridge didn't wear bathing suits and that someone belonging to our little family party lost a priceless pocket knife out of the car window. I forget now which one of us owned the pocket knife. I can only remember that it was priceless, also that it was irretrievably lost.

After awhile we reached Virginia City, which was a wonderland to a small boy. They had real Indians there, with four kinds of paint on their faces, and the big mines fumed and puffed and roared all day and all night. Fierce-looking white men carried pistols strung to their belts, and mild-looking yellow men, with hair strung out like the tail of a kite, carried baskets to and fro.

The town clung to the side of a mountain, and probably because there were plenty of stones lying about, the small boys took up as an amusement the accomplishment that made David famous. They, however, found no Goliath. This was bad for the yellow man with the basket. His was vicarious atonement, but his salvation was slow and only came when the offending boys grew out of the habit. Then, as a rule, an entirely new band of Davids took the field.

At the mature age of six years I ran away. My destination was Gold Hill, which was ever so far away—almost a mile. I had a new velvet suit on, my best cap and shoes, and I had ten cents in money tied up ever so tightly in the corner of a handkerchief. I started out bravely, but I never reached Gold Hill. A heavy rain had preceded my departure from home, and although the storm was fully over and the sun was shining, I encountered a pond of ocean-like proportions before I had gone a block. I tried to ford it, slipped, and fell. Between mud and water my new velvet suit gained pounds in weight, and when with the assistance of a neighbor I had scrambled out of the pond on the side nearest home, I had no heart for further journeying.

As the years passed I grew friendly with the Indians. Among the redskins who passed through Malley's lot, which lay beside my home, was one who, though wearing a bandana for a bonnet and keeping up to the fashion of calico gowns of loud pattern, had the stride of a man. I first noticed that neither buck nor squaw had any respect for the mystery. It always walked at the last of the file and rarely did anyone speak to it. In time I learned that the mystery was once a brave who went forth with his tribe to battle the greedy white man. His mistake was that he broke and ran at the first fire. The rest of the tribe waited for at least another volley. After the fugitives had traveled a score of miles, taking about two clumps of sagebrush to a leap, they held a powwow and gave the brave who had had the unpatriotic hurry a choice of death or woman's clothing for the rest of his days. He hurried into a dress and had been a human scarecrow for a dozen years when I last saw him. This made me think that the Indian isn't as fond of dying as some writers have made him out to be.

I shall always remember my first school teacher. I can understand her now. She was a great-hearted little woman, who refused to believe that boys are savages. School for the week ended on Friday afternoons, and after the boldest of us had spoken pieces from the platform—Friday being the day for exercises—teacher took up a position in the narrow doorway, intending to kiss each of us as we passed out. She got along lovely with the girls, but with the boys, who, to her idea, were not little savages, it was different. They took notice that the teacher did not fill the doorway, and then they sneaked through and trickled through and rushed through, and when such schemes didn't work they formed a flying wedge and upset her. She never succeeded in kissing more than ten percent of the boys, despite the fact that our fathers advised us to submit; but still, she never would agree with anyone who called us savages.

Outside of school—to use the language of the small boy— "slews of things" happened, but if I don't stop the flow of reminiscences soon I shall be writing a book.

Before I cease, let me record the fact that I once thought myself worthy of a halo. The great hoisting works of one of the Comstock mines near my home caught fire; the flames leaped along until the whole structure was ablaze and the shower of sparks threatened the destruction of every house within a quarter of a mile.

When my people began to move household goods down the hill, I ran into the house and rescued the family Bible. I did not look for anything else. I was a self-conscious hero, and I confidently expected that my picture and a thrilling story of my deed would appear in the Sunday school papers. Really I felt disappointed when the fire died down and I had to lug that big book up the hill again.

With that failure of the fire to at least damage the house, my hope of fame was gone. I knew then that it was my last chance. No Sunday school paper has ever printed my picture. After the fire, life was never the same for me. The incident made a great difference in my early career. I groped along with a sense of injury for a few years. Then I began to feel grown up, and of course, what has happened to me since then isn't worth telling.

# COMMENTARY

*Prejudice against the Chinese laborers, reflected in Johnny and his friends, burned hot in the breasts of the miners when William E. Sharon, promoter of the Virginia and Truckee Railroad, hired several hundred former railroad coolies to work along the right of way of his road in 1869. He was in a hurry to complete the railroad in order to carry Comstock silver to the mills along the Carson River. The miners feared the next step would be to put coolie labor in the mines, threatening the four dollars a day pay which had been negotiated by the Miners' Union in 1867. The coolies toiled unmolested on the railroad through the summer, but in the early fall of 1869, while they were industriously laying grade between Carson City and the American Flat tunnel, miners from Virginia City and Gold Hill came down in force, drove the Chinese away, and destroyed their living quarters. Only when Sharon promised that no Chinese would ever be hired in the mines were the men willing to let the coolies resume work on the railroad.*

*This deep distrust never subsided, and as the production of the mines dwindled, anti-Chinese sentiment increased, and children of the Comstock heard much talk about sending the Chinese back to China. In Johnny's time the boys stoned, not railroad coolies, but another breed: the Chinese who lived down on the only natural flat in town, just northeast of the railroad station and a little below D Street, where the light ladies had lived in the sixties. These Chinese bothered no one, leaving their narrow-laned shacktown only to gather and sell wood (digging out the very roots of the trees early miners and the Indians had overlooked), peddling the bundles of faggots from the backs of burros; or to gather laundry (which they dried on their roof tops); or to serve as cooks and houseboys in the mansions and hotels up on the mountain side.*

*Both the* Virginia Evening Chronicle *and the* Territorial En-terprise *frequently carried stories criticizing this practice of ston-ing the Chinese, especially by half-grown "hoodlums" who were seldom punished.*

*The squaw man who mystified Johnny was probably a veteran of the first Battle of Pyramid Lake, fought on May 12, 1860. He must have been around for nearly twenty years when Johnny last saw him. The battle, fought under the leadership of Young Winne-mucca, when his father, Old Chief Winnemucca, refused to make war, was one of vengeance on the part of the Indians, and included some five hundred Piutes and Bannocks.*

*The trouble began when hired hands at Williams Station, a Nevada stop on the Overland route, captured a couple of young Indian women in the absence of the station owner, and mistreated and imprisoned them. When the husband of one of the young women tried to rescue them, a fight followed in which the Indians killed the molesters and freed the women.*

*Without waiting to learn the reason for the Indian attack on Williams Station, more than one hundred men from Carson and Virginia City, under the leadership of Major William M. Ormsby, founder of Carson City, raced out in search of the Indians, whom they found waiting near Pyramid Lake.*

*Seeming to retreat after a few shots, the Indians lured the white force into a narrow ravine and trapped them there. The survivors of the resulting near-massacre ran for their lives. One Indian was said to have waved a flag of truce just before the battle began and was fired on instantly by the whites. He disappeared in haste. Perhaps it was this bid for peace which caused the warriors to sentence the Indian in calico dress to be a squaw for the rest of his life.*

*The hoisting works fire started at seven-thirty on the evening of January 12, 1881, when Johnny was a little more than ten years old. A lamp had exploded in the miners' changing room of the Hale and Norcross, one of a number of mines toward the south end of town. Flames spread rapidly, aided by ubiquitous zephyrs blow-ing a fierce gale. Several shifts of miners working on both the 2,100-and the 2,400-foot levels were cut off from escape by the fire at the top of the Hale and Norcross shaft. They were ordered to get away through the tunnel into the Savage mine at the 2,400-foot level and to come up through the Chollar-Norcross-Savage shaft. By nine o'clock all the men were safe on the surface. By midnight, the Waldorfs had taken their belongings, including the heavy Bible that Johnny had "saved," back to their home. The main mine building, the hoisting engines, the top of the shaft, and the compressor engine were all reduced to blackened wreckage. The hoisting works were never rebuilt, and the Hale and Norcross miners thereafter used the shaft by which the men had escaped during the fire.*

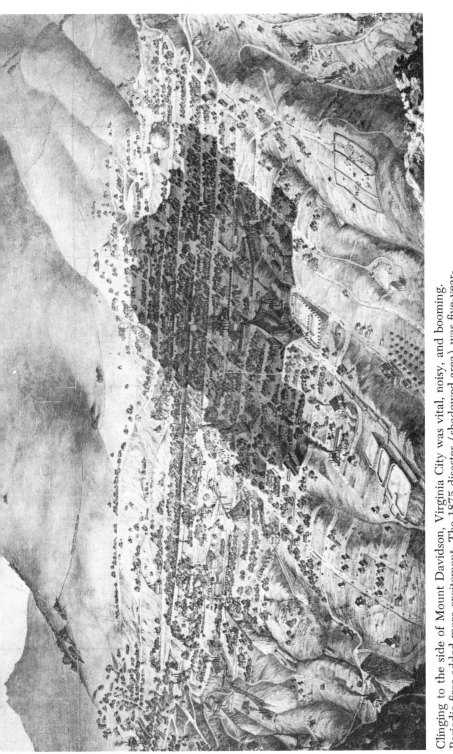

Clinging to the side of Mount Davidson, Virginia City was vital, noisy, and booming. Periodic fires added more excitement. The 1875 disaster (shadowed area) was five-year-old Johnny's first. "It was better than a circus," he recalled.

Virginia City, as seen from above the road leading to the Geiger Grade, with the First Ward School at center left. For young Johnny Waldorf "the roaring frontier outside the classroom made school the dullest place in town."

The Comstock that Waldorf knew as a boy of eight. The International Hotel is at center right, with the Con-Virginia mine beyond. Steam rises from the Ophir and Sierra Nevada mines.

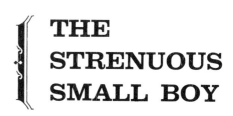

# THE STRENUOUS SMALL BOY

TO BE RAISED in a mining camp means an experience as full of thrills and wounds and scars as going to the wars. You who have tried it and have survived its perils deserve service medals. If I ever meet Andy Carnegie, I'm going to speak to him about it. I want a piece of that kind of junk myself.

It would be easier for me to tell what didn't happen to me in Virginia City than to tell what did. I wasn't more than ten years of age when I got my first peep into the barrel of a revolver. Behind the artillery—it looked like a cannon to me—was a somewhat excitable gentleman from the Azores.

There had been a fire the night before, and, kid-like, I was poking around among the remains of what had been a second-class shanty looking for something to play with. I surely didn't want to play with the owner. He didn't want to play, either. He borrowed the speed of one of his bullfighting ancestors and came at me. As he closed in, he obligingly lifted the gun so that I could see into it, uncoiled a string of Portuguese oaths, and topped it off with as vigorous an invitation to "Get out!" as I ever heard. I got. Was I frightened? Maybe not. Frightened didn't mean anything to me in those days. I was scared. As far as I know, I still hold the white ten-year-old championship record for climbing close-boarded seven-foot fences.

About two years later I helped myself to a worse scare than that. Some of my grown-up friends were prospecting in an old tunnel that in a wandering, drunken way had sought to touch the heart of the mountain. One morning they yielded to my "Lemme go with you," and into the tunnel we went. For several hundred yards it was fine Whenever I wanted to, I could turn my head and see daylight.

Then the tunnel turned and got smaller and smaller until even I had to stoop to keep from bumping my head. The candles threw a bilious light a few feet ahead of us, and we had no trouble in keeping to the car track that ran the length of the tunnel.

I turned my head to look for that circle of sunshine. All was blackness. A wall of coal couldn't have matched it. Dark nights were noonday compared to it. I stepped on the heels of the man in front of me in my eagerness to keep up.

After the dark had followed us along that sluice-like tunnel for a few minutes, we reached a station, a widened-out place where two other tunnels joined ours. One of the men told me that if I took the tunnel to the left, which came in at a deceptive angle, making it seem a part of the main tunnel, I would walk straight into the Savage shaft, which didn't go more than two thousand feet below the level on which we stood.

We moved on, with me in the center of the group, and in perhaps ten minutes we reached another scooped out place. Here we took a ladder route and reached the gallery in which my friends had been working. It wasn't bad there, except when I was foolish enough to think that the earth above us might decide to cave in. With much difficulty I made this thought keep its distance.

After a while I grew hungry. The men weren't going out for two hours yet, they said. I dreaded to make the trip alone, but I couldn't wait that long. One of the men hinted that I was afraid to go by myself. That settled it. He lent me two inches of candle, and I said, "So long, fellers," and went down the ladder.

After I got into the tunnel I never looked back, but stooped and hurried on whistling as hard as I could. A whistle wasn't much against a big silence like that, but I had to do something. I got along fine for about five minutes, and then my light went out. My heart gave a great thump. My hand went feverishly into my pocket. Not a match! My knees shook.

If I groped on in the dark I might get into the wrong tunnel and be dashed to death in the Savage shaft. If I stayed where I was and waited for the men to come out, like as not they would have a car ahead of them and it would come speeding along the down grade, drowning my cries of alarm and crushing me to death when it reached me.

Perhaps there would be room for the car to pass if I hugged the timbers close, but I didn't dare to risk it. Then, again, I felt that two hours in that black silence would make me an old man. I muttered prayers, and stammered as I prayed. I thought of my prized possessions—twenty-seven marbles, including nine crystals and two agates; two tops, a boxwood and a "Frenchy"; a "redhead" baseball and twenty cents in money. I would have given them all for a match. Shivering, I went through all my pockets. In a corner I found half a match. Joy unimaginable! It was the wrong half. Despair unspeakable! I dug into the pocket again and found a hole. In that hole, stuck deep in the lining, I found the other half. The hand that held it flapped like a bird's wing.

Finally I steadied down a little, and then I tried the match. The flame flickered. I could hardly hold it to the candle. The candle flickered. The flame steadied, and I gave a deep sigh that almost put it out. With nervous joy I went on again. That light was my life, and I guarded it carefully.

I reached the station. That black hole to the left was the Savage tunnel. I breathed easier after I passed it. At last I came to the turn. It was all easy now. I could see that circle of light again. I dropped my candle and never stopped running until God's sun was shining on me. I didn't go into another tunnel for a week, and then I had matches in sufficient quantity to make a candle merely a convenience.

As to the wounds and scars, they came from climbing around ore houses and up the beams of trestles and over the great waste dumps. A fall a week was a fair average. It seemed as if we were trying to see who could fall the farthest and live. When it was reported that Jimmy Dillon had fallen forty feet, "Spider"

Walker measured the distance with his eye and remarked dis-
gustedly, "He ain't done nothin' to brag about. 'Taint more'n
twenty feet."

I had more than my share of falls. The oddest mishap of all
occurred one afternoon when the wind was busy carrying loose
shingles from the town to any old place down the canyon. I had
a sack of shavings from the Savage carpenter shop and, as I
came down the dump, dared to walk in the teeth of the wind
out on the roof of the G Street tunnel, intending to drop the
sack into the road below to save carrying it a little part of the
distance. That sack of shavings served as a sail. The wind
caught it. I held on, and the sack and I took a trip together.

I landed on the rocks, and a neighbor's boy carried the shavings home—to his home, not mine. After I got well, I had many
an argument with the boys over that fall. The tunnel was sixteen feet high. I explained that I fell about four feet sideways
before I began to drop, but they would never give me credit for
falling more than sixteen feet.

# COMMENTARY

*All of these adventures were recalled off the cuff, as it were, by a
busy reporter preoccupied with special assignments and with no
time to verify dates. His memory erred by several years in telling of
the adventure with the Portuguese householder.*

*Johnny was two months and nine days past his eighth birthday
when on July 11, 1878, several buildings down in the next block
on South H Street burned during the night. (Perhaps the man regarded eight years as an impossibly tender age for such an experience since his eldest had just reached nine years during the summer
of 1905.)*

*The fire, the first after a long interval in a fire-conscious town* *(it was not quite three years after the Great Fire of 1875), apparently began to burn around midnight, but was not discovered until several hours later. It was in a vacant building at 172 South H Street. Since the $450 insurance policy on the building was due to expire on July 12, there were some dark suspicions hinted at by the* Territorial Enterprise.[1] *Whatever the cause, the flames spread to several shanties and small houses, among them the building next door to Manuel Jassie's place. He and another family were renters.*

*In the building on the far side a miner's wife and her five children slept in spite of the shrieking of the Savage Mine whistle above them. It was not until the fire came through the walls into the mother's bedroom and crawled into bed with her that she and her brood awoke and escaped in their night clothes.*

*More alert, Manuel Jassie had saved some of his belongings, which were stacked near the smoking ruins when Johnny came over the back fence to see what he could see, which turned out to be the business end of Mr. Jassie's revolver. According to the* Enterprise, *Mr. Jassie, whose dwelling was a total loss, saved only a little furniture and had a personal property loss of about $1,200. No wonder Johnny saw the round eye of that gun as he snooped around what little the poor man had saved.*

*Virginia City was honeycombed by tunnels, some dug for exploratory prospecting operations, some for water so badly needed before the great siphon system built by San Francisco engineer Henry Schussler was completed in 1875. This system brought sweet, pure water from the Sierra across the Washoe Valley and over the mountain to Virginia City.*

*Although the tunnel described by Johnny connected with the Savage Mine, it was much too close to the surface to have been anywhere near the Sutro Tunnel, which connected with the Savage at the 1,640-foot level.*

*Perhaps these older friends of Johnny's were from the growing ranks of the unemployed; there were many in the late seventies and eighties, so many that Virginia City newspapers ran stories warning the unemployed from elsewhere not to come to the Comstock.[2] There were too many skilled miners with families looking for what jobs Virginia City might have to offer.*

*Either the reference to the "G Street" tunnel was a typographical*

*error in the issue of the San Francisco* Bulletin *running this recollection, or it referred to a roofed-over cut made through the Gould
and Curry Mine complex when the railroad was extended to the
new depot near Union Street. The old depot stood just south of the
tunnel coming out by the Gould and Curry works. When the railroad was extended from the old to the new depot after the Big Bonanza was discovered in 1873, the E Street tunnel was cut through
to bring the line close to the Con-Virginia, scene of the great find.*

*When the Virginia and Truckee was built in 1869, it took three
tunnels to carry the line from Gold Hill to Virginia City's old
depot. One went under Fort Homestead while the next almost paralleled the Old Tunnel Road through the Divide. The third may
have been that roofed-over cut near the Gould and Curry, but in
1875, right after the Great Fire, a long story in the San Francisco*
Chronicle, *said to have been written by Dan de Quille, told of the
tunnel between the old and the new depots as having been burned
out.*[3] *This was the E Street tunnel. For a time the old depot, south
of the Gould and Curry, was used both for passengers and freight
until damage from the fire could be repaired and another depot
built. Remnants of the E Street tunnel are still visible today when
looking south from the old freight depot, all that remains of the
terminal. The mouth of the tunnel has been filled or caved in but
the scar of it is still there.*

A good illustration of "square-set" timbering invented by
Phillip Deidesheimer, which made mining in the Comstock possible.

MINING
ON THE
COMSTOCK

Drawn by T.L.DAWES. 1876 – Copyrighted 1877.

PUBLISHED BY
J.B. MARSHALL, GOLD HILL, NEV.

Shaft house of the Savage Mine, Virginia City.

"It is as if a wondrous battle raged," J. Ross Browne once said of the Comstock. "Myriads of swarthy, bearded, dust-covered men are piercing into the grim old mountains, ripping them open, thrusting murderous holes through their naked bodies." In 1867 Timothy O'Sullivan, official photographer for Clarence King's Geological exploration of the fortieth parallel, captured a few of those "dust-covered men" in the shaft house of the Savage Mine (overleaf). Later he descended to the depths and used a flash of magnesium to take the first underground mining photograph in history (above). "Miners of the Comstock . . . seemed to know no medium between stolidity and passion," wrote Eliot Lord in *Comstock Mining and Miners* (1883). The former mood was on man and boy in this group picture (right) taken at the head of the Utah shaft.

# KINGS
# OF THE
# COMSTOCK

VIRGINIA CITY and its famous Comstock Lode were responsible for half a dozen millionaires, including the quartet of Bonanza Kings—Mackay, Fair, Flood, and O'Brien. We children of the camp heard of them all, but only two of the "awfully rich" made any impression upon us. These two were James G. Fair and John W. Mackay. The others might better have been myths as far as we were concerned. In that event we would have given them at least an occasional thought.

In my day Mackay and Fair were familiar figures on the Comstock. Neither came to town any oftener or stayed any longer than business demanded. Fair had a mansion up on B Street. If Mackay ever had a residence in the camp in my time, I never knew it. Fair's visits were frequent; those of Mackay were few and at long intervals, but we children learned to dislike Fair and to look upon Mackay as the kindest man in the world.

The millionaires were known to us by their first names. Like our fathers, we spoke of Jim Fair and John Mackay. By keeping our ears open while our elders were talking among themselves, we heard much that was not to the credit of the one and formed our opinion on those tales. Our opinion of the other was based on the personal experiences of numerous small boys.

It didn't matter where one went if the object was to learn what the kids thought of John Mackay. The Divide Gang, the Andes Gang, the First Ward Gang, and the C. C. Gang differed on a great many things, but every member of all four gangs would tell you that John Mackay was all right.

We used to envy Fair his wealth. Mackay couldn't have too much to suit us. We naturally supposed that each had more than a million in good hard coin. If any one had told us that about all their wealth was the mines, on the dumps of which we wore out our shoes, we wouldn't have believed it. Millions with us meant actual money, aside from such trifles as mines and mills.

This view of things gave that mansion on B Street an attractiveness that it should not have possessed. We believed that it contained heaps of twenty-dollar pieces. Just where the heaps were located was a favorite subject of speculation. All of us had at one time or another got a peek into some of the big rooms with the great chandeliers and rich carpets and gorgeous furniture, but the money wasn't in sight. As none of us had ever been in either the cellar or the garret, we concluded that it was in one of those two places. This narrowed the scope of the argument, but whenever as many as three of us took up the subject, there was no chance of agreement.

I shall never forget two of the many stories that were told of the master of the mansion. There was a poor old miner who had injured his back so badly that he could work no more and became a charge on the county. He lived in a little cabin and was able to do his own cooking and washing. For firewood he depended on the carpenter shop of the nearby Savage Mine. The foreman of this shop, a man named Jim, always responded to the old man's request for blocks and shavings, sending them over to the cabin.

One day when word came that the old man was out of firewood, Fair happened to be "nosing" around the works. The foreman, being something of a diplomat, dispatched a carpenter to find Fair and lay the matter before him. Fair stroked his beard as he listened to the story of misfortune. When it was ended, he did the right thing but in a way that robbed it of the charm of benevolence. He took his own good time to get around to the carpenter shop, and when he reached the foreman he said, "Jim, send a load of blocks to that broken-backed pauper."

The other story is still worse. There was a strict rule against smoking underground. No one objected to the rule, for the reason that a fire in a mine generally meant the loss of many lives, but still not a few of the miners were willing to menace their safety and their jobs to get a few pulls at a pipe.

One day while Fair was on one of his lower level inspection tours, his keen nose caught the smell of tobacco. Without making any remark as to his discovery, he turned to the miner at his side and said longingly, "I'm dying for a smoke. I'd give anything for a pipeful of tobacco." The miner looked up, but Fair's face gave no hint of suspicion. Fair spoke of his longing again and again. Finally the miner took pity on him, reached behind a timber and brought forth a pipe and tobacco.

Fair took a smoke, but when he got above ground he made it his business to see the foreman and say, "Fire that man; he's smokin' down there." It wasn't so much what Fair used to do as the way he did it. I don't wonder that we kids didn't like him.

It won't take long to tell why we used to think so much of John Mackay. In the first place he had a pleasant pastime habit of scattering money among the gangs of small boys who used to hang around the mines. This, however, wasn't the main thing. His claim to our affections was based principally on what he did whenever he went to the theater in Virginia City.

Each performance in Piper's Opera House meant forty or fifty penniless small boys hoping for miracles as they stood outside the entrance. Old John Piper would sit in the box office and scowl at us until his fat face was all wrinkles. Then Mackay would come along, nod his head toward the gang, and say, "John, how much for the bunch?"

A heavenly smile would wreath John's face as he counted us and announced the result. At fifty cents a head it generally came to about twenty dollars. Mackay would say, "Let the kids see the show," and John would deal out our tickets with one hand while he gathered in the twenty with the other. We would enjoy the show, and what is more we would think better of all mankind because John Mackay had remembered that he was once a boy and had given us something from his great store.

That is why we never envied John Mackay. We wanted him to live forever and always be rich. When he died, we children of the Comstock, although most of us had not seen him for years, felt that we had lost a near and dear friend.

# COMMENTARY

*John W. Mackay and James G. Fair were both living in Virginia City when Johnny began tagging along after the big fellows in the Savage Gang. The homes of both men had been destroyed in the great fire of October 26, 1875.*

*Mackay never replaced the pretty bay-windowed cottage up at Howard and Taylor Streets, but Fair rebuilt further down the mountain side on South B Street. It was a stately, two-story white mansion surrounded by an elegant garden and fence, and it still sits majestically on the west side of the street. Here his shift bosses used to come in the evening to report and consult, and here he fumed and worried and tossed and brooded about what might be going on down in the mine until Mrs. Fair and his doctor prevailed upon him to resign as superintendent on July 10, 1878.*

*After the fire Mackay moved into the offices of the Gould and Curry Mine not far from Johnny's home and kept house there with a Chinese servant until the new International Hotel was completed in 1877. Thereafter, he made his headquarters on the top floor of the hotel whenever he returned to Virginia City. Mrs. Mackay preferred Paris to Virginia City.*

*James C. Flood and William S. O'Brien never had lived in Virginia City. The profits of their partnership in the Auction Lunch down in San Francisco had financed their first speculations in mining stock. Long before they joined forces with Mackay and Fair, they had become rich stockbrokers. They gambled all the money they could lay hands on to back Mackay and Fair's hunch* that the elusive Comstock Lode was down somewhere in the Con-Virginia. In no time, Mackay and Fair proved they were right, and the four Irishmen became the Bonanza Kings.

The four men, Mackay, Fair, Flood, and O'Brien had come to California in the gold rush when poor Irishmen with little education were enduring the intolerance of many Americans, especially the Native-Americans or Know-Nothings. It was a shock and an affront to such people when these four men outguessed, outsmarted, and outclassed everyone else on the Comstock, including shrewd William E. Sharon, and proved that the lode was not played out in 1873. Of the four, only Flood was born in the United States—and he was the son of poor Irish immigrants.

Mackay and O'Brien never let their millions blind them to old friendships. They were kindly men with natural grace. Flood became suspicious of most men, disapproved of Mackay's generosity in giving away millions in "loans" or outright gifts. Flood repulsed all but the well-screened visitors who managed to get past his inquiring clerks and through inner office doors with trick locks. Only Fair seems to have given back contempt for the condescension and intolerance that any Irishman had to endure in the years after the great migrations of the 1840s.

While there were more than 800 Irish miners working in the mines and the Sutro Tunnel in the seventies and eighties, according to Eliot Lord, there were working with them 1,601 Americans, Canadians, and English, besides other nationalities.[1] Mine superintendents learned that it was better, for temperamental reasons, to mix the nationalities in every shift. The mines employed only the most skilled men because of the flat four dollars a day wage set and maintained by the Miners' Union. Teamwork and compatibility on every shift were essential.

The four Irishmen who became millionaires many times over were regarded with more critical judgment than might have been given more rooted Americans in a similar situation. It was hard for prejudice to down. So the talk Johnny heard about Fair could have often enlarged his eccentricities. None, including Johnny's father who worked as a shift-boss in the Con-Virginia, could ever have said that Fair was not a good miner or an able manager. Fond of machinery, Fair installed the best equipment in the mines, both

*for safety and for efficiency. He never asked the miners to do any-
thing he wouldn't and couldn't do and spent many hours down in
the hot depths with the workmen. Fair's reaction to the need of the
crippled miner for stove wood bespeaks a rough man, but if his
wealth had been less unbelievable and he had not risen from a pick-
and-shovel Irish miner to arrogance, he might have been referred to
tolerantly as a diamond in the rough.*

*The injured miner obviously was a member of the Miners'
Union. No man could work in the mines without joining the union
as soon as he had earned the price of the initiation fee. As a union
member he had no doubt received his eight dollars a week benefits
for ten weeks of at least the first year. Benefits did not start until
two weeks after the injury and had to be certified by both a doctor and
witnesses.[2] According to Dan de Quille in* The Big Bonanza, *mine
managements also provided benefits if the accident were not due to
carelessness. Families of miners killed in the line of duty received
benefits from the union.*

*The story of the miner who smoked against rules is similar to one
related by Oscar Lewis in* Silver Kings. *In the latter case, an entire
shift was fired by Fair after the men had all offered him the makings
of a smoke. Fair passed the blame on to Mackay, which none of the
miners would have believed, knowing Mackay. He would have found
some way to punish offenders for such flagrant disregard of safety
rules without costing them their jobs.*

*The story of the horrors of the Yellow Jacket fire in Gold Hill in
April 1869 should have been enough to remind any man of the
hazards of carelessness with fire. It broke out early one morning,
spread to the nearby Kentuck and Crown Point mines, brought
agonizing death to forty-five men, burned for days, and smouldered
noxious gases for weeks. As late as two months after the fire, men
collapsed from those gases and were carried unconscious to the
surface. Months later, picks were still digging into smouldering
beams. Three years later, red hot rocks were found. No one could be
sure, but it was believed that the fire started when a miner's candle
was carelessly left stuck in a beam of tunnel facing.*

A line drawing in *Harper's Weekly* recorded the changing of the shift at Consolidated Virginia. A later version below.

# GREAT MEN
# I HAVE KNOWN

IT HAS BEEN MY FORTUNE to meet several boastful gentlemen who had much to say about the great personages they had known in their childhood. One had been chucked under the chin and called a nice boy by General [Ulysses S.] Grant; another had almost been run over by James G. Blaine's family carriage; and a third had been danced on the knee of Henry W. Longfellow. To tell what happened to the rest would be what the schoolmen called superogation.

The boastful gentlemen referred to have given me many a pang. They swung famous names as though they were clubs and flattened me out completely. I did not dare to say that I, too, had known great men, for if I had done that, I would have had to explain that they were great despite the fact the world did not know them.

At least they were great to me, who looked upon them with the guileless eyes of a small boy. Why should I care for the jeers of the boastful gentlemen? Perhaps they are drawing on their imagination for most of the familiarity of which they are so proud. I can tell the truth about my great men. To think is to act. I shall be browbeaten no longer.

"Old Doc" was the first great man to come into my life. If I ever knew his other name, I have forgotten it. He, like my other wonderful friends, lived in Virginia City. His cabin clung to the slope at the lower edge of the town and was in the midst of an acre of sagebrush, which Doc called his garden. He was as careful a housekeeper as he was a gardener, and the one room of what he named in his grand way "the mansion" contained large quantities of unfashionable bric-a-brac, most of it heavily coated with plebian dust and dirt. I used to marvel at the durability of the washable arabesque work on the dishes that he used at his meals and once plucked up courage to ask, "Why don't you wash your dishes on the outside?"

He hadn't been "baching" for twenty years for nothing. I knew that from the answer he gave me. "Don't worry, Sonny," he said. "If I ever find any use for the outside, I'll do it."

What school Doc graduated from I was never able to find out. It was said of him, however, that he was skilled in his profession and had given a new lease on life to more than one world-weary mining camp mule. When I knew him, he didn't have much practice, and he used to spend a great deal of his time telling stories to the children who flocked around his cabin door.

They were marvelous stories, and I feel ashamed of myself as I vainly try to recall even one of the many that he told in that dry, cynical way of his. He added to his greatness by giving us candy and nuts, even though he carried them in the same pocket with his tobacco. Sometimes he made us happy, and sometimes he made us sick, but we loved him and looked up to him; and when the railway company came along with a sidetrack that blotted the cabin from the landscape and drove Doc into exile, I was sorry enough to cry. Still I didn't cry. Instead I turned my affections to another great man.

"Uncle Jimmy" was my new idol. His last name was Anderson. I am sure of that. He, like Doc, lived in a cabin, but his domicile stood in the midst of a nondescript collection of houses and had no garden of sagebrush. Uncle Jimmy was an old man, and he was everybody's uncle, though he had no money to lend even on the best of security.

He often told the grown folk that he had had money once but had favored a minister of the gospel with seven hundred dollars, without taking even a scratch of the pen to prove the debt, and the minister afterward amassed a competency and laughed at his unwise creditor.

Although the tragedy in Uncle Jimmy's life was twenty years in the past and had happened three thousand miles away, all Virginia City knew of it and understood why the old man hated preachers. Uncle Jimmy told us stories and made us gifts, and he, too, was a great man.

He was on the list of the county's indigents and was given twenty dollars on the first of every month. Part of that meager sum added to the happiness of the children of the neighborhood, and with us Uncle Jimmy ranked higher than the mining millionaire who lived in the most wonderful house in all the town.

To the credit of our idol, he never even hinted to us that he hated preachers. He told that to our elders, and we learned of it by keeping our ears open when we were supposed to be occupied with the dreadful homework that was part of our school course. Even then it was hard to believe that the old man's heart was full of bitterness. When we were around, it seemed that he loved the whole world.

In time blindness came to our dear friend. He took his affliction patiently and grew more gentle with each passing day, but from what our fathers said to one another in our hearing, we knew that the "sky pilots," as Uncle Jimmy called them, were not forgiven.

One morning the cabin door was not opened at the accustomed time. A little later a neighbor climbed through the window and found the old man groaning on the floor. His life was almost over, but he wanted no physician. No one dared to speak of the need of a spiritual comforter.

The day dragged on, and while the children tiptoed around the door, Uncle Jimmy grew worse. We could hardly believe our ears when we heard him groaning over and over again, "The Lord have mercy." We thought of his hatred of ministers, of the fiery pit, and shuddered. At nightfall one of the neighbors came hurrying out of the cabin and cried, "Run for a priest!"

I was off in an instant, never stopping to take breath until I reached the Church of St. Mary-in-the-Mountains. The priest ran faster than I, but when he reached the cabin, Uncle Jimmy was dead. That night there wasn't a child who knew him who didn't ask the Lord to be kind to our friend who had gone.

Colonel Ed Boyle was the third and last great man of my boyhood days. I met him first one bright summer's day shortly after I had been taken with the notion that I was old enough to run away from home and make my own way in the world.

Without a cent in my pocket, I had walked straight past the schoolhouse and started along the road to the Geiger Grade that ran downward to Truckee Meadows and freedom. I hadn't gone more than a quarter of a mile when Colonel Boyle came along in a buggy. He picked me up and wanted to know where I was going. As he knew my father, I didn't dare to tell him that I was bound for Reno and the transcontinental railroad that led both ways to fame and fortune.

I explained that I was just going out to the tollhouse, about a mile ahead. He put me down there and went on, but no sooner had he disappeared around a bend than I was following his wheel tracks.

All morning and all afternoon I trudged along in the dust, growing wearier and hungrier every minute. Reno was twenty-two miles away, and at sunset I had still half a mile to go and didn't care much whether the town in sight was Reno or Timbuctoo. I was disgusted with life.

I heard the sound of wheels coming toward me but did not look up. Suddenly a kindly voice shouted, "Whoa!" The vehicle stopped, and someone said, "Aha, running away, eh?" It was Colonel Boyle. "I used to do that myself," he added soothingly. "There's nothing in it. You better jump in here with me."

I got in, and we started home together. All the way he told me stories of his boyhood. Why, although his hair was gray, he was still a boy! When we got to the foot of the grade, he stopped at Floyd's roadhouse and had me supplied with a loaf of bread and a large wedge of cheese. Never since that day have I tasted bread and cheese as sweet as that. It gave me courage to face the jeers of the neighbor boys. As for Colonel Boyle, I still believe that he was the greatest man I ever knew. God rest him:

# COMMENTARY

*Uncle Jimmy[1] was probably James Anderson, a miner who lived near the Hale and Norcross dump in the early seventies. By the latter part of the decade he had no occupation and lived at 148 South H Street, not very far from Johnny's home.*

*Colonel Edward D. Boyle,[2] known as Colonel "Ned" Boyle to Virginia City editor Wells Drury and others of his contemporaries, had arrived on the Comstock in 1863. He worked as a miner in the Imperial before he rose to become superintendent of the Alta Mine in Gold Hill. Later he was superintendent of not only the Alta but the Washington and Benton mines. He was the father of Emmet Boyle, later governor of Nevada.*

*The school Johnny passed so defiantly was probably the Third Ward School,[3] down near the Catholic church. It stood where the town's very first school had been built in 1862. The tollhouse stood about two miles from the center of town and probably was the one later known as the Collins Station Toll House.[4] The Geiger Grade,[5] for which Dr. Davison M. Geiger and J. H. Tilton obtained a franchise from the territorial legislature in November 1861, became an extension of the main highway from Truckee and Lakes Crossing in 1863. Associated with Geiger and Tilton in this enterprise, which connected the Truckee country with Virginia City, was L. H. Torp, who became tollhouse-keeper at the Virginia City end shortly after the Virginia and Truckee was completed. It was then that Dr. Geiger, who had kept the tollhouse himself, went off to build more highways, finally to invest in mines and prospect around Bishop, California. One day in his seventy-fifth year Dr. Geiger was found lying dead in the sage after his riderless horse returned to the old man's cabin alone. Torp was county commissioner for eight years before his death in a runaway accident in December 1878. He, Geiger, and Tilton are all commemorated at the Geiger Lookout[6] on the present Geiger Grade. From this eminence one can look down to the left on the faint markings of the original Geiger Grade, which plunged down Newton Canyon two thousand feet in five miles.*

*The Five-Mile House[7] stood that distance out of Virginia City and near the point where the first grade turned and sheered off west to make the descent into the canyon. Since Johnny made his last runaway down that shadowy canyon, the road has been realigned three times. It was first paved in 1933. In the late seventies when Johnny probably made his first attempt to run away, the grade was narrow and hazardous. The boy tramped on down the winding way past Hairpin Turn and Dead Man's Point, scenes of many a freighting accident, holdup, and runaway; and on past Madden's repair shop, where two of the first locomotives[8] of the Virginia and Truckee had been stalled in 1869 along with twenty oxen, which had been trying to pull them up the grade to Virginia City. Johnny had trudged beyond the valley tollhouse and Steamboat Springs, probably well past Granville M. Huffaker's ranch and station on the railroad before Colonel Boyle spied him on his return from Reno.*

William C. Ralston

Silver turned the world of the Comstock and speculation became a way of life. It could create a king, like the sternly regal William Ralston (overleaf); build a palatial mansion, like J. C. Flood's "Linden Towers" (left) and even stop the meditation of old Adolph Sutro in his San Francisco library (below).

# TRUTH AND THE INDIAN

ELLING THE TRUTH ABOUT INDIANS seems to be a hard
task. To one writer they are "noble red men," to another
they are "merciless savages." One would have you believe
that the swarthy American freeholders are transplanted Spartans; the other would convince you that if you gave an Indian
a thousand dollars in coin he would show his gratitude by shooting the gift into your diaphragm a coin at a time. This, of
course, does not imply dissatisfaction with the gift. According
to the authority on "merciless savages," it is merely an evidence
that pure cussedness holds a twenty-four-hour-a-day grip on
the Indian and never takes a holiday.

During the years that I knew the Piutes, I loved Indian
stories. When I was ten I read "Mocassin Mose," "Long Abel,
the Scout," and numerous other thrillers telling of bloodthirsty
savages, and liked them immensely. I never knew a Piute to
harm paleface man, woman, or child, but this made no difference. We children were wiser than our elders when we divided
Indians into two classes—those that we knew and those that
we read about. Sometimes the Indian we read about was noble
and sometimes he was merciless, but the Indian we knew was
neither. He thought a little of the Great Father and more of
ease and choice provender, in which respect he was not unlike
the untanned folk further up the hill.

There was a certain dignity about the Piute buck, but it was
not born of nobility. It would be hard to determine the cause

of his pride. I used to think that it grew out of a feeling of superiority due to a realization that the white man couldn't get along without working. Perhaps this was so. The fact that a few bucks occasionally unbent to the limit of saving and chopping wood for the whites does not disprove my theory. The lapses referred to were voluntary and were prompted not by necessity but by a desire to get money to play poker.

In fancy I can see the patchwork tepees among the sagebrush. Trees were scarce, and the skeleton of the wonderful habitation was invariably of castaway pieces of pipe. Over the pipes were spread sheets of the kind of muslin known as house lining, sacking, pieces of carpets, and, in fact, fragments of everything available that would serve to keep warmth in and cold out. There was nothing new to the structure. All was secondhand and came from the whites.

The fire in the center of the tepee was confined to an old stove rejected by the hill folk, and the smoke rose through the regulation stove pipe. Not all of the smoke escaped this way. Some of it emerged at the dents where the lengths of ancient pipe joined and helped to make life interesting for the family circle. Around the battered stove, with its cracked lid, the whole family slept with feet to the fire.

In Virginia City every buck save one was called Jim, and every squaw was either Mahala or Mary. Only the chief had a distinctive name. Every baby was a "papoose." When the family came uptown, Jim always led the way. I used to wonder what would happen if some ambitious Mary ventured to catch up with her lord and master.

The single file order of procession grew dreadfully monotonous, but it troubled only the onlooker. Mary trudged along patiently carrying the painted papoose on her back, also everything else that had to be carried, and seemed content with her position. The only social concession that I ever knew to be accorded her was the proud privilege of sitting in a poker game with a bunch of shiftless Jims who had made a few dollars hunting ducks, geese, and jackrabbits for market.

This always happened after Mary had done a hard day's work up the hill washing clothes. The Jims wanted her money, and they always got it. It was rather delicate of them, I thought, to resort to poker instead of using force.

The Piute's love of poker seemed his greatest passion. He took the white man's game and varied it by a cross with casino, which was known as Indian poker. We children learned by observation and used to play Indian poker with matches. In time it became the custom in many houses to keep the matches under lock and key. This, however, is a digression.

The Indian always played for hard money. Nothing could keep him out of a poker game except lack of coin. When Captain Bob, chief of the Piutes, lay dying, a buck was hurried after a priest. He ran as hard as he could for a quarter of a mile. Then he struck a poker game, sat in, and played for three hours. That was as long as his money lasted. Then he ran the other quarter of a mile to the church and delivered his message to the priest. By this time Captain Bob had been dead two hours and three quarters.

To the youthful mind the Piutes were good for just one thing. They supplied pine nuts, of which the white children were fond, and it wasn't necessary to have money to make an exchange. Jim was all ready to trade pine nuts for sugar, coffee, or candles. It was just as well to trade these things for pine nuts; in fact it was the right thing to do. Otherwise Jim would beg them from you.

The Piutes were the only people I ever knew who could beg with dignity. It made me feel in debt to them every time I gave them anything. Jim never seemed to be begging. He just stood up and asked for what was coming to him. Mary wasn't quite so impressive. She prefaced her begging by pressing her greasy, painted face against the window to see if the family was home.

The first time Midget, having just arrived in Virginia City in 1905, saw such a face peering at her through the window, she silently fainted.

# COMMENTARY

*Two cultures were fighting for survival on the fringes of that Comstock mining town when Johnny was a boy, the Amerindian and the Chinese. The Indian was fast losing out. The struggle was over wood—to sell and, if there was anything left, to warm their hovels.*

*The trees that once grew on the mountainside had been worked over three times, first by the early miners cutting wood for supports to brace their exploratory tunnels, then by the Indians in search of firewood to peddle, and finally by the Chinese, who had even grubbed out the very roots and taken the sage and wrapped it in bundles.[1] In the boy's time the mountain was barren, stripped clean; it was not until recent years that new growth of cedar and juniper began to make a sizeable showing.*

*The Chinese wood peddler was far craftier than the Indian. He knew how to make twenty faggots look like a bundle of thirty, and the price of the lot went up as the temperature went down.[2]*

*By the seventies, the Indian began stalking from door to door, looking for woodpiles to cut into stove lengths while his squaw looked for clothes to wash. Even then, the Chinese had a much more marketable method than the Indians; they picked up the laundry and trotted with it down to their wash houses. It came back clean and neatly folded.*

*Poker was indeed a serious occupation for the Piutes. Even old Chief Winnemucca, who was in his seventies when Johnny was a youngster, could never resist a poker game. Dan de Quille wrote as fact that Winnemucca had been known to lose his ponies, blankets, guns, and clothing at poker, coming out of the game stripped.[3] Indians never gambled with white men, but it has been said that what the Indian learned about white men's ways was learned from the criminal and the outcast, all bent on getting the most out of him.[4]*

*The use of metal pipe in the construction of the Indian tepee, or wickiup, came about as a result of the great fire of 1875.[5] Until October of that year the Piutes had used willow poles for the supports of their cone-shaped dwellings. From the hill above, they*

*looked like clusters of tilted beehives. The old photographs testify
to that: little huddles of hives covered with tatters.*

*It was a long walk all the way to the Carson River to find willow
poles. Some observant Indian noticed the twisted gas pipes lying
in the debris after the fire and tried an experiment that quickly
caught on. An* Enterprise *reporter discovered in April 1878 that
nearly every wickiup down below St. Mary's Hospital and south
of the county graveyard had taken on a firmer contour, but the
coverings still looked as if they had been picked up by nesting spar-
rows. The Piutes had learned how to bend the longer, sturdier
lengths of pipe into the proper shape, thrusting one end into the
ground and using the more slender pieces to fasten into ribs lashed
to the uprights with scraps of wire.*

*Captain Bob, a tall, rangy Piute, lived in this settlement below
the hospital, just a nice walking distance from the Chinese cemetery.
But Captain Bob did not live in a wickiup. He had a shanty of
wood furnished by the county commissioners. It was the conviction
of Sam Davis, reporter for the* Virginia Evening Chronicle *at the
time, that Captain Bob died at thirty because of the house and the
stove that kept it warm. Apparently, the chief died of tuberculosis.*

*Moses, a Piute medicine man, had treated Captain Bob with
various Indian remedies, which ranged from herb brews to dancing,
smoking, meditation, and incantation. But Captain Bob got no
better. Finally on Sunday, February 8, 1879, two hundred Piutes
gathered at Silver City to decide whether or not to stone Moses to
death. They seemed to suspect that some of the herb brews were
poison.*

*Although Sam Davis was fond of Captain Bob and sympathized
with the plight of the Indians, exiles in their own land, he could
not resist making a bigger thing of what seemed a good story. He
insisted that the Indians had listened to the plea of Moses that since
a medicine man was entitled to five deaths among his patients before being stoned, he was still two to the good, for so far he had lost
only three. They decided to defer action until later.*

*But on Saturday, February 15, Davis found Captain Bob far
gone. His bow and arrow had been laid across his breast and his
squaw and little children were lamenting pitifully.*

*Commenting on the Indian distrust of Moses, Davis wrote,*

"*When an Indian was informed by a* Chronicle *reporter that there were some doctors in Virginia who had been killing one man a month regularly for some years, he expressed his unbounded astonishment and passed some very profane and uncomplimentary remarks on the stupidity of a race which would submit to such imposition.*"[6]

*The year before Captain Bob's death he had been converted to Christianity, and Bob and his family were all members of Father Patrick Manogue's parish. There is no doubt that someone was sent at all speed over the hill to St. Mary's and that the nameless someone had not returned; nor had the priest, a good friend of the Indians, put in his appearance when shortly before two o'clock Captain Bob was seen to be in his last throes.*

*It was then that Sam, his half brother and heir to his title, leapt up and away, racing desperately to the church. In a very short time, Father Manogue's gigantic frame was seen coming down the hill at a long striding clip, his cassock flying, his hands full of the necessary sacred symbols of the last rites. But poor suffering Captain Bob had already left for the happy hunting ground.*[7]

*Services were held next day in the Catholic church. When they were over, Father Manogue led the procession north to the cemetery, his rich robe of office swinging with his long stride, his lips moving in prayer.*

Enroute home from a triumphal round-the-world trip, ex-president and General Ulysses S. Grant visited the Comstock in 1879. Among those welcoming him were silver kings James G. Fair (far right) and John W. Mackay (far left).

Water—along with heat, foul air, and gas—was the miner's deadly enemy. It was fought on the Comstock with bigger and bigger pumps as mines burrowed deeper and deeper. Shown here is the mighty Union shaft pump.

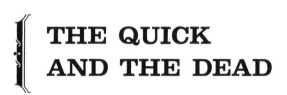

# THE QUICK
# AND THE DEAD

Y OU VIRGINIA CITY BOYS of the old days, let me ask you a question: didn't we use to have great fun whenever we went over the hills to the Chinese cemetery? We didn't think anything about human beings taking their last rest, did we? What we did know was that the "Chiny buryin' ground" was a good place to go when we didn't have anything else to do.

Except on funeral days and the annual gathering and scraping of bones preparatory to shipment to China, we could chase squirrels and run and jump and play leapfrog all over the patch of ground which the Chinese were seeking to free of evil spirits.

We used to follow the funeral cortege with broad grins on our impish faces. Prayer papers, thrown to the breeze by the mourners in the hope of outwitting the curious devils who follow the Chinese dead, kept dropping at our feet and flying in our faces, but we didn't stop. According to the rules, devils can be relied upon to waste time in deciphering the marks on the prayer papers, thereby enabling the man in the hearse to get a long lead in the race for the cemetery, but we trooped right along regardless of both superstition and decency. Occasionally one of us grabbed a prayer paper on the fly, and the rest of us shouted in chorus, "Good catch."

We keenly enjoyed the last sad rites. The "Chiny buryin' ground" didn't seem like a cemetery to us. There were no trees, no flowers, no marble headstones. Other cemeteries had these things, but the space set apart for the Chinese was merely a bare place on the hillside. Unpainted pieces of board took the place of headstones, and in most instances the names were written in pencil. A few of the graves were enclosed by unpainted fences. To us the whole place was still part of the hills, and so we didn't feel the least bit wicked when we sat back in the sagebrush and made merry.

As the wagonload of eatables was piled upon the newmade grave, we passed remarks upon the bill of fare and wondered if the spirits didn't get tired of a steady diet of roast pork, roast chicken, and rice. One of us would say, "I ain't hungry, but gimme the wishbone." Another would assume an air of wrath and announce that he was going to fire the cook. Still another would say something equally foolish, but it sounded all right to us.

It must have sounded differently to the Chinese. Two or three times they charged on us and sent us flying over the hillside. In fairness to the gang it should be stated that the disorderly retreat was not due to cowardice. We drew the line at one thing. We wouldn't throw stones at a funeral.

There were others who found enjoyment at the Chinese cemetery. The Piute Indian, who was born hungry and has never been able to satisfy his appetite, looked upon a Chinese funeral as something that fate had arranged for his particular benefit. At one time half the bucks of the tribe did little else save watch for signs of a coming of the procession that wound up with the commissary wagon. They didn't care for the music, but to them the food was manna from heaven.

In order to conceal his sinister design, the Piute generally waited for the procession and scowled as it passed him. This was his idea of diplomacy, but it never occurred to him that the scowl always relaxed when the banquet wagon came along. The smell of the food set his nose quivering with baseborn delight, and his face suddenly took on what a Piute would probably call a smile.

Behind a clump of brush on some nearby hill, he waited impatiently for the mourners to leave the cemetery. As soon as they took the road for town, he made a detour, approached the graveyard restaurant from the rear, sat himself down, grunted,

"Ugh! Heap good!" and pitched in. He always had plenty of company. Sometimes he got generous and brought his family along. Even the chopsticks were found useful. They were given to the little papoose to play with. The squaw squatted down a few graves away and humbly took what was passed to her.

It was a great tribute to Chinese cooking, but the diners didn't care for rice and by throwing it away brought about their own undoing. For a long time Chinatown believed that spirits had eaten the food. Why the rice was neglected was something the Chinese couldn't understand. It was good rice and well cooked, but the dish that contained it was invariably found bottom-side up and the food scattered on the ground.

At first it was thought that the spirit was eccentric. Then some skeptic started an investigation, and one day after a big funeral a score of Indians were surprised in the midst of a banquet that was the Piute social event of the year. As a wag remarked, they were caught red-handed. From that time on, the food was guarded, and when after a few hours it failed to disappear, it was loaded into the wagon again and taken back to Chinatown. Thus ended the golden age of the hungry Piute. Since then life for him has been one long yearning for a square meal.

With the elimination of those wonderful feasts, the Chinese cemetery lost one of its principal attractions, but the small boy still found it worth a walk over the hills. The digging up and the polishing of the bones of the departed had a fascination for us, and we used to sit on a hill a little way from the scene and think what a fine joke it would be on rich relatives in China if the diggers and polishers should mix the bones of a merchant and a rag picker. After it was all over and the workers had departed, we would wander among the graves, gather a punk or two and a few prayer papers, and go home happy, thinking only of what a fine thing it was to live within walking distance of a "Chiny buryin' ground." And still cynics persist in referring to Christian small boys as little heathens.

# COMMENTARY

The route to the Chinese cemetery which Johnny and his unmannerly friends followed most was apparently down Taylor Street, past St. Mary's, and around back beyond the county graveyard. It was quite a walk from Johnny's home on South G, as it was the equivalent of about twelve blocks. Traveling was probably heavy, for the road was certainly not paved.

There is said to have been another Chinese cemetery over beyond the Sierra Nevada dump, a little removed from the Eureka Society's cemetery. But the Chinese graveyard had left no more evidence there than over by St. Mary's. The white marble stones of the Jewish cemetery now peer from among the sage and the rising cedar grove almost in the shadow of the dump.

On January 18, 1879, a very elaborate Chinese funeral procession went down Taylor. The Chronicle reporter estimated that it had cost all of six hundred dollars. No name was given for the deceased, but he was described as a "prominent Chinese Mason." He may have been the wealthy Chinese merchant who kept store in a brick building on the edge of Chinatown, where Virginia City boys bought firecrackers.

An American brass band boomed at the head of the funeral procession, followed by fourteen Chinese mourners in full regalia. The leader wore a very voluminous black and red muslin robe and may have walked on stilts, as he was described as "big." Following the official mourners came the hearse and directly behind it a shrill squirling Chinese band, which, to the occidental ears of the reporter, made bystanders "envy the corpse." Last of all came an express wagon filled with "varnished hogs." Such delectable fare was not always provided for the departed. More often than not it would be cold ham, turkeys, and chickens.

At the rear of the procession, yet keeping a cautious distance, were observed a "contingent of hungry Piutes." The reporter opined that there would doubtless be Indians foraging in the Chinese graveyard that night.[1]

An antidote to isolation and a commercial boon, the tenacious little Virginia and Truckee railway linked "Virginia" with stamp mills along the Carson River. One engine could manage the twisting downward trip, but more were added for the steep haul homeward, as seen above. Breathtaking Crown Point Trestle (below) loomed 90 feet high and 250 feet long.

# LET'S GO
# TO THE FIRE!

DID YOU EVER RUN A MILE to a fire and then feel keenly disappointed because the firemen had everything under control when you reached the scene? If you never did, you must have had a queer sort of childhood. Did you ever view a fire merely as a spectacle, without any thought of what it meant to the victims? If you never did, you were born grown up and had no childhood at all.

Years ago in Virginia City we small boys didn't think much of firemen except on the Fourth of July, when they turned out in red shirts and were the hottest thing in the whole parade. On this particular day we were ready to forgive all our enemies in our love of garish display, and we forgot that the firemen had robbed us of many a bully time by putting the fire out just when things were getting interesting.

My first fire was something to be remembered. I recall with regret the inability of the firemen to master it before it had desolated two-thirds of Virginia City, but I wasn't sorry the day it happened. I was five years old then, and the thought that hundreds of people were losing their homes never occurred to me. The fact that my own home didn't burn probably had much to do with the perfection of my enjoyment.

The fire began on the hump of ground between Virginia City and Gold Hill known as the Divide, swept northward for nearly a mile, then turned eastward and leaped downhill until the gaps between houses became too great for the flames to bridge.

A quarter of the city remained intact, and in the center of the spared section I stood surrounded by furniture that had been removed from structures which had been menaced all day by a shower of sparks.

I can still shut my eyes and see the clouds of smoke and the blinding sheets of flame. In fancy I can follow the fire as it raced along the uptown streets. It was the greatest day of my five years of life. Around me I could hear men shouting orders to women and see women wringing their hands; but the sea of flame made my eyes dance with excitement, and only a yell in my ear or a heavy hand on my arm could have made me think of anything else. I did not know the word then or I should have called it magnificent. The flames crackled and roared. The world seemed to be burning up, but somehow I had no fear, and the boys around me were equally callous. It was better than a circus.

When the fire reached the group of churches on Taylor Street, everybody was in a frenzy, grown-ups as well as children. I learned then that it took something more than belonging to a church to make people good. When the first of the three churches began to burn, men and women belonging to the other two seemed just as happy as I was. They didn't think the fire was going any further. When it took a sudden leap and enfolded the second church, only the people belonging to the third were happy. The third church was almost all brick, and everybody thought it was safe, but it wasn't. Soon the flames began to creep up the steeple, which was wood and burned beautifully, and then of all the watchers around me only the children were happy. All churches looked alike to us, especially when on fire.

It was a great day. Not until night were the flames brought under control, and when at last I was tucked away in bed, I was still smiling. Many a little boy was without a home, but we heathens of what was left of Virginia City never thought of that. We had seen something to delight the vandal heart of childhood. We had drunk deep of the joy of it, and nothing could rob us of our recollections.

In the days that followed the big fire, I was kept close to home. The clouds of smoke rising from blackened ruins recalled my day of happiness, but no one took me to see what uptown looked like after the flames got through with it. I had to stay down on G Street and listen enviously to the stories of other boys who had gone sightseeing through the burned district. My personal knowledge of the aftermath was extremely limited. About all I can remember now is old Sam Wagner, the Negro town crier, going slowly along F Street ringing his bell at short intervals and shouting: "Nevah despair, good people, nevah despair. The kind folks ob Reno and Carson hab come to your rescue, and dar's loads of pervisions at the depot."

I got Mother to translate Sam's message of glad tidings. When I asked her what part of the "pervisions" was coming to our house, she pointed to the full cupboard in the corner and explained that only those who had been burned out could share of those good things at the depot. If my memory doesn't fail me, this information made me regret that we still had a roof over our heads.

When I attained the mature age of eight years, I began to go over the back fence whenever I heard the big bell in the Corporation House sound the first tap of a fire alarm. This was partly haste and partly diplomacy. It averted the risk that goes with asking permission. Sometimes I got so thoroughly warmed at the fire that it really wasn't necessary for Dad to warm me again when I got home. Then there were the disappointments I had to undergo. More than half the fires weren't worth seeing —some of them just chimneys burning out, and four times that I remember the firemen spoiled everything by driving back flames that were only beginning to creep out on the roof. They might have let it burn a little while, but they wouldn't. Firemen never seem to realize that a boy has to have some fun once in a while.

One day I came pretty near starting a fire that would have made history for Virginia City. I was sitting in the changing room of the Con-Virginia waiting for Dad. Before me was a hot cherry-ripe stove. I got busy with my feet and surprised myself by kicking the stove over. The cherry-ripe iron set the wooden floor ablaze. I was scared from my tow hair to the tips of my copper-toed boots. I could imagine the great hoisting works wrapped in flames, miners losing their lives, and everybody in town running after me with a rope. The picture was too much for me. I let out a yell that was lost in the clang of machinery. Then Dad and another man happened in and put out the fire. The loss to the mining company was something less than two dollars. The scare I got was worth a thousand.

Two or three almost fireless years dragged by. Then a portion of Chinatown took fire, and everybody was happy. The firemen didn't work very hard that day, and a breeze would have meant effective Chinese exclusion. Eight or ten stores and houses left nothing much behind save the odor of smoldering punk sticks, but I wasn't satisfied. I had hoped to see the joss house go up. We boys wanted to know how the broad-faced, scowling idol beyond the rice bowls would behave under fire. He escaped the test, and most of us went home and either kicked the cat or tied an oil can to the dog's tail. That made us feel better, but we couldn't get it out of our heads that something was wrong with the firemen. I know what it was now. We used to think it was the business of a fireman to make work for himself.

# COMMENTARY

*Frontier towns were always tinder for fire in the days of coal oil lamps, candles, and flimsy muslin-lined interiors with wallpaper covering. Virginia City was especially vulnerable because of the fierce tornado-swift winds, whimsically referred to as "zephyrs," which swoop down the mountainside and burst out in twisting whirlwinds and powerful gusts that even today can do considerable damage to a carelessly opened car door. More than once a frolicsome zephyr has carried flaming tumbleweed, burning muslin, wallpaper, and tufts of glowing mattress stuffing through the air like missiles from an ancient catapult, firebrands that menaced the dwindling town as recently as 1942, when more historic relics of glory disappeared.*[1]

*On the morning of October 26, 1875, everything was at its worst for Virginia City. The mountainside was parched and dry and the wind blowing a gale when at the end of an all-night drinking brawl in the rooming house of "Crazy" Kate Shea up on A Street between Taylor and Union, someone knocked over a coal oil lamp. When the lamp exploded and sprayed flame in all directions, Kate and her befuddled guests fled, leaving the fire to get a good healthy start.*

*It was between five and six o'clock in the morning, and within twenty minutes of the outbreak of the fire, Dan de Quille saw twenty to forty buildings in flames.*[2]

*The great fear among mine owners and miners alike was that the fire would find its way down the shafts and do the same horrible damage that had been done at the Yellow Jacket in Gold Hill back in 1869. In 1876 all the miners in Virginia City were out of the depths in time, and all immediately joined bucket brigades or dynamite corps to fight the fire. Among them at the Con-Virginia was Johnny's father. They threw a bulkhead of earth over the mouth of the shaft and fought the flames shooting along the trestle to the mill. John Mackay worked with the men, shouting orders and heaving buckets of water.*[3]

*When fiery shingles from the roof and steeple of the brick Catholic church began flying in the direction of the Con-Virginia, Mackay called for dynamite. Father Manogue, who had been a miner himself and knew what a mine fire meant, may have protested (it is not recorded), but he knew what must be done. His beautiful church, just seven years old, would have to go.*

*A horrified, weeping old Irish woman staggered to the Con-Virginia and pleaded with Mackay to spare the church. He looked up long enough to see that the depot was gone, that flames seemed to be consuming the Ophir and were roaring through mountains of mine timbers stacked for the unending job.*

*"Damn the church," he shouted through the uproar. "We can build another if we can keep the fire from going down the shaft."*[4]

*It was estimated that it took no more than three and a half hours for the fire to destroy a large part of Virginia City.*[5] *When the fury was over and only smoking debris lay where the flames had roared,* the city fathers began blaming the water company, and the water company blamed the city fathers. The water company made a practice of shutting off the main valve at the reservoir at six o'clock each night and did not turn it on again until six-thirty the next morning. When the fire broke out between five and six o'clock in the morning, consequently, there was no water in the hydrants. And by the time someone made it up to the reservoir, there were no hydrants and very little equipment left in Virginia City.[6] Most of the cisterns were soon emptied. Only that of the Gould and Curry remained to save the southern mines and the part of town where Johnny lived. When it was all over, the water company blamed the city fathers for not providing enough hydrants—there were six. Later, fire hydrants appeared on every corner.

Within a week, the fire-blighted town was swept by a heavy snowstorm. Then a few days later, a fierce wind that even the zephyr-hardened residents described as a "tornado," blew down the brave, partially rebuilt frameworks. But they went up again, and Dan de Quille thought the sight seemed like new patches on an old pair of pantaloons.[7]

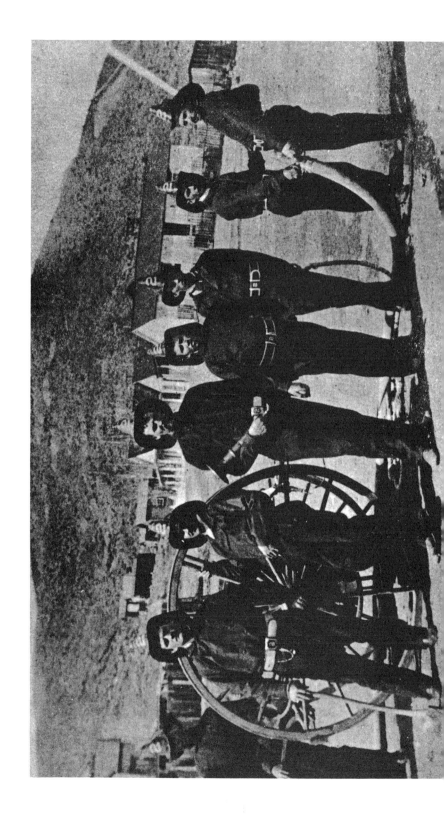

Virginia City was especially vulnerable to fire because of the fierce, tornado-swift winds, whimsically referred to as "zephyrs." Above is the stalwart hose crew of the ever-ready Young America Engine Company No. 2. Fire prevention on a volunteer basis was a matter of civic survival, but it provided an opportunity for good fellowship as well. Left, the members of Company No. 4 put on a show of hands.

# HOORAY FOR THE FOURTH!

NOWADAYS ONE FOURTH OF JULY seems to follow close on the heels of another. It was different in the old days. Somehow the Fourth of July used to approach Virginia City with the most irritating leisure. Perhaps we began to look for it a little early, but as nearly as I can remember, we always waited until the middle of May before we began to count the days. At any rate, "Old Doc" stretched the truth when he said: "Them Arctic Circle fellers haven't the best of us. We split our year into two days, and have a heap more noise, 'cause one is Christmas and the other's Fourth of July."

The period of anticipation always tried our patience sorely, but the necessity of getting our own spending money took some of the edge off the dullness. It was a poor day when we failed to gather something in the way of junk. We accumulated bits of wrought iron, cast iron, lead, zinc, copper, brass, and glass. We saved up coal oil cans, sacks, and rags. Our mothers had all they could do to keep us from stripping the house of extra clothing. Rags were quoted at half a cent a pound, and the last week of the long wait always found us looking upon everything in the cloth line as rags. Once a boy whose name has escaped me was a little short of the twenty pounds that the junk man demanded before he parted with ten cents, and he made up the difference by "nipping" his mother's wedding dress. She never wore it, and he couldn't see what use it was anyway. Father was big and strong. There wasn't going to be any stepfather, and sister had vowed she would die an old maid rather than wear a second-hand wedding dress.

This brings up a picture of Robinson, the junk man. He was tall and had curly hair and a sharp nose, and he carried ever so many dimes and quarters and halves in a dirty leather sack. Maybe he wasn't tall, but he certainly looked big to us. He had a yard piled high with junk, and we gave him a financial rating second only to that of Mackay and Fair. In the matter of arithmetic he was a genius, except on the rare occasions when he smelt of whisky.

With Robinson there were only two perfumes in the world, whisky and onions. The latter never interfered with his talent for driving keen bargains. The former generally got him badly mixed, but when he paid more than was due, the boys who were acquiring Fourth of July money were too patriotic to remind him of his error. Robinson was not a philanthropist, and he prided himself on his business ability. Perhaps the boys didn't want to hurt his feelings.

Giving credit where credit is due, I, on behalf of the kids of the old Comstock, admit a debt of gratitude to Robinson. He had the only junk store in town, and if he had spurned us, many a fine Fourth of July would have been gloomier than the first day of school. Money from that dirty leather sack was responsible for much enthusiasm and more noise. The money that came from home always had a string to it. We were expected to spend it like little gentlemen; what we got from Robinson's we scattered around in ways that would bring the most joy to our heathen souls.

Fourth of July was a day of early rising. We used to get up before the sun lit up the streets, but not before the beams had begun to caress the flag on Mount Davidson. The splendor that the Stars and Stripes borrowed from heaven made our hearts beat with a fierce patriotism and filled us "chock full" of a brand of enthusiasm that meant trouble for the timid, nervous folk who dreaded redheads, bombs, and doubled-headed Dutchmen.

I shall never forget those doubleheaders. They have since been outlawed. They were the Captain Kidds of fireworks. We aimed them carefully and touched them off. With an honest explosion they started on their journey, flew straight to the victim, and at the critical moment completed their usefulness by another explosion louder than the first. When a Virginia City boy sighted an enemy on the Fourth of July, he bought a quarter's worth of doubleheaders. After the quarter's worth was gone, the enemy owed the boy something.

The parades of those old days! They were worth seeing. The town had more kinds of soldiers than Napoleon ever marshaled under his banners. The Emmet Guards in the glory of Irish green with soldierly Captain Peter Dunne at their head; the Washingtons in red, the Nationals in blue, the Montgomerys, the Sarsfields, the Tigers, the battery of artillery, three or four brass bands, plenty of color, plenty of noise. It was glorious.

Of course, we had our favorites. Some of us wanted to be Emmets, but it was the Tigers who caught most of us. The Tigers wore zouave uniforms and had a color combination of red and blue and yellow that was irresistible. It was once the ambition of my life to be a Tiger. If I had succeeded, I would have slept in the uniform. I would never have had the heart to take it off.

Aside from the soldiers and the brass bands and the red-shirted firemen, we small boys found nothing in the parade worth noticing, but there was plenty of what we wanted and we were thankful. The grand marshal and his arm of aides, the floats, and the ship of state with a stuck-up Goddess of Liberty and a bunch of giggling girls had little interest for us.

Once Dr. John. B. Zangerle, the "Flying Dutchman," wore the sash of an aide and rode the meanest horse in town. He was an exception. "Doc" charged up and down C Street; the horse shied about twice a minute, and the parade had to do some lively sidestepping. As far as I know, "Doc" is the only marshal's aide who ever made a hit with the small boys.

And now the Fourth of July is coming again. How the day can be properly observed without the Emmets, and the Montgomerys, and the Washingtons and the Sarsfields, and the dear old Tigers is beyond me. They are all gone. Still, the country is free. I can't understand it. Perhaps I'm getting old. Yet I'm young enough to shout, "Hooray for the Fourth!"

# COMMENTARY

*Considerable superstition was attached to Johnny's dawn-kissed flag at the top of Mount Davidson. It was more than a symbol of national pride to the people of Virginia City. It was their hope of another bonanza.*

*When a gale blew the old wooden flagstaff down and shattered it during the stormy winter of 1877/78, there was dismay and foreboding throughout town. Members of the old Eagle Engine Company No. 3, whose proud duty it had been to raise the flag on the mountain top each Fourth of July, immediately pledged themselves to the raising of money for a new flagpole. "We shall never have another good strike on the Comstock until our flag again waves at the masthead on top of our guardian mountain," lamented an emotional veteran of the old company. "Stocks have been soft ever since the old flagstaff fell."[1]*

*The collection of money for a new and stronger successor to the old flagstaff began very shortly after its demise, but times were hard and it went slowly. As soon as the snow had melted sufficiently to make the climb, Jack Magee of the Delta Saloon hired a group of men at four dollars a head to climb to the top of the mountain and bring back a length of the old pole to be cut into souveniers and sold. They made it down with a twelve-foot length. But by late May, only half of the necessary three hundred dollars needed had been subscribed. Hearts were warm, but pockets were pinched.*

*In early June Andrew Peasley and Thomas Alchorn were still collecting. Most people gave a dollar and were assured that if there were any money left after the flagpole had been installed, the balance would be turned over to the Fourth of July committee. There was to be a metal box sunk in concrete at the base of the staff, in which a list of all who contributed to the fund, as well as newspapers of the day and any "articles of interest" that citizens might like to include were to be sealed.*

*The cast-iron flagpole that was finally financed was a tremendous*

*affair, eighty-four feet, seven inches in length; the globe to sur-*
*mount it weighed eighteen pounds and was two feet in diameter.*
*Six horses, panting and pulling in the eight-thousand-foot altitude,*
*dragged the pole and its globe to the top of the mountain on Friday,*
*June 21.*

*The staff was to have been installed on Sunday, June 23, but the*
*men had trouble getting it to stand in a perpendicular position. The*
*breeze must have been a big factor although the weather had been*
*balmy enough for wildflowers to carpet the mountain side. Tents*
*and awnings had been provided for the ladies, and at one time*
*seven hundred people had made it to the mountain top, only to wait*
*in vain. It was not a climb many wanted to repeat very soon, and*
*through the night old timers seeing the camp fires burning on the*
*peak were reminded of the signal fires of the 1859 Piute troubles.*

*It was not until July 2 that the flagpole was finally secure in its*
*moorings. The* Enterprise *noted that Lincoln D. White, a hardy*
*artist, was on hand to sketch the flag as it rose, and the California*
*Mining Company cannon was primed for the salute. The hundreds*
*waiting on the mountain top realized their hopes at last when the*
*new flag, a gift of "Colonel" James G. Fair, rose to the tip of the*
*tapered pole, then snapped open with the breeze. Down in town the*
Enterprise *broke into a headline, "There she blows!"*[2]

*The Fourth of July celebration when Johnny Waldorf was eight*
*was typical of Virginia City. The California Pan Mill down in*
*Six-Mile Canyon flaunted its new electric light at the top of the*
*works until the sun rose. Father Patrick Manogue not only promised*
*that the fountain would spray from the top of St. Mary's steeple,*
*but that if someone would provide the price of "a display so mag-*
*nificent," it would "spout champagne."*[3]

*Owners of milk wagons promised to carry ice along the line of*
*march for participants overcome by the July heat. The route they*
*traveled was traditional for many years: "along B Street to the*
*junction of B and C on the Divide, thence down C Street to Carson*
*Street, thence west along B Street to Piper's Opera House," where*
*the procession would be "reviewed and dismissed."*[4]

*The memorable moments of the parade, according to the* Enterprise, *were provided by Captain Bob's half-naked Piutes and by*
*Gilrooney, the town scavenger. Told that he would get a dollar a*

head for every Piute he recruited for the line of march, Captain Bob showed up with fifty Indians, all "painted with spots, stripes, and zig zags of white."[5] They tapered down from six-footers like Captain Bob to little boys of five or six, and they marched in single file led by Bob on his pony. Sam Davis has described Captain Bob's habitual mount as a mule so short that the big Piute had to bend his knees to keep his huge feet from scraping on the ground. No doubt the pony was loaned for the occasion, as Bob's own mule was lame, minus an ear, and possessed of other infirmities. Captain Bob proudly carried a gleaming, naked sword. It was his last Fourth of July procession.[6]

Gilrooney the scavenger with his two weirdly costumed dogs brought up the rear of the parade, mocking all the participants that had gone on before and clowning his acknowledgment of the cheers.

The National Guard Shooting House, Virginia City.

"The parades of those old days!" Waldorf recalled. "They were worth seeing. The town had more kinds of soldiers than Napoleon ever marshaled under his banners." Above, the Emmett Guard marches down C Street on the Fourth of July.

# WHO'S GOIN' SWIMMIN'?

W HEN FATE CONSIGNS the small boy to a place where he can't go swimming, she robs him of half the joy of living. We youngsters of Virginia City never imagined that the world held such unfortunates. When the hot weather came on, we made a run for the C and C pond and peeled and dived. That is, most of us dived. I was a bit awkward and invariably went in with a flop.

All small boys know that the weather gets warm long before the water does. The bolder spirits among the gang always forced the season, and the first one in could count on an admiring throng watching him from the bank.

Besides being a hero, our gallant leader was a juvenile Ananias. Whenever any of us asked him, "How's the water?" he answered, "Fine," even though his teeth chattered so he had to divide a one syllable word into three. We noted the chill that affected his conversation, but as soon as we became convinced that he could take the plunge and live, we followed his example. Then we realized what a liar our hero was. Chunks of ice couldn't have made the water colder. This made a few timid souls clamber out in a hurry. Then the rest of us set up a stuttering shout of "C-c-cow-ard." About two shouts was our limit. The chill and the kicking and splashing in an effort to get warm left us little breath for shouting. After a while exercise took the edge off the cold, and we had what a small boy calls a "bully swim."

I was one of the little fellows in those days, and as the big fellows swam in the same pond, our joy was mixed with trouble. The big fellows chawed beef on us. Many a time when a cold wind was sweeping along the bank, I came out to find my shirt tied in a hard knot. While I shivered and struggled with the knot the big fellows laughed at me and inquired, "Hey, kid, why don't you hurry?" Still the torture had some compensation. It gave my hair a chance to dry and enabled me to go home without the circumstantial evidence which never failed to tell Ma and Pa what had happened.

This was a good thing for me because the impression prevailed in the family circle that I was born to be drowned, and when I asked to go swimming, Dad had an unpleasant habit of singing a verse that I had learned to dislike. It went something like this:

"Oh, Mother, may I go out to swim?"
"Oh, yes, my darling daughter;
"You may hang your clothes on a hickory limb,
"But don't go near the water."

I wasn't a darling daughter, and Dad couldn't sing any better than I could, which meant something unique in the way of discord; but his meaning was plain, and therefore anything that brought about the drying of my hair before I started homeward was a blessing, though it came in a most forbidding disguise.

The mere thought of those hours in the old pond makes me young again. Such diving! And "fetching!" And treading water! The art of "fetching," called by spectators swimming under water, was held in the highest esteem, and the boy who could disappear under the water and make the length of the pond without coming up for breath was envied by his fellows.

The best I could do was to make it sideways, and at that I sometimes spoiled the dramatic effect by plowing head on into the mud of the other bank. According to the story of observers, I also offended by sticking my feet out of the water at frequent intervals and making a splash that suggested the performance of the whale they had seen in the picture books. Some of those fellows seemed to think that I could breathe through my heels.

There were other joys less difficult than "fetching"; I can

still hear the boys shouting, "Bet you can't touch bottom," and see the challenged youngster throw up his hands, hear him shout, "Here goes," and see the water rippling where he went down. In a few moments he comes up, shakes the water from his head, and cries triumphantly, "I did it." We had to take him at his word. There was no going behind the returns.

Something else that I recall was not a joy. We used to go in and out several times in an hour, spending the intervals sitting on the bank or running up and down in the hot sun. This meant a bad case of sunburn. Only swimming is worth such suffering. Sometimes for a week our backs were so tender that a touch would set us jumping in agony, and when a sunburned small boy got a "lammin'," he knew a torture such as Dante never dreamed. I had the experience, and I know.

Memory makes a picture of the old pond, and I see the big hoisting works nearby, and the great dumps, and the hospital on the hill. At the foot of the hill and hidden from our view lay the brewery. One day while we were gathered on the bank lazily getting back into our clothes, a man came along with an empty lard bucket. "Where's the brewery?" he asked. No less than four of us solemnly pointed to the hospital. "All right, kids," he said, and proceeded to go all wrong.

He was a hard-looking citizen with a large foot that wouldn't have hesitated to stir a small boy's conscience, and while he was making for the hospital we were breaking all records for donning attire. The first boy dressed started off at a run. I followed with one shoe on and the other in my hand. The rest of the fellows came trailing along, looking as though they had been rescuing clothes from a burning laundry. Just before we got out of sight of the misinformed stranger, we took a hasty glance, and there he was, marching confidently up the hospital steps and swinging the bucket with jaunty ease. I heard afterwards that he fought the janitor and got licked before the thought dawned upon him that he might have been deceived.

We were always curious to know if he reached the brewery and filled the can, but although we saw him again, it was at a distance just right for safety, but too far for speech. It's too bad we didn't have telephones in those days.

The C and C wasn't the only pond, but it was the bathing resort most popular with the small boy. There were warm water ponds near some of the mines, but they were not deep, and anyway it takes cold water to put life into a swim.

I never knew but one warm water pond that ever did anybody any good. This one was below the Norcross dump, and the water was hot enough for dancing. Captain Bob made use of it once when a Piute buck had loaded up with fire juice and was threatening massacre. Seven volunteers lured the bad Indian from the warpath and, at Captain Bob's word of command, tossed him into the Norcross pond. He screeched and whooped and did a war dance never excelled in the Piute country. The spectators liked it so well that they wouldn't let him out. After a while Captain Bob relented, and a meek and sober Indian crawled from the pond. He had taken a fifteen-minute jag cure but it was fifteen days before he felt well enough to sit in a poker game.

Indians are only an incident. They have nothing to do with the great sport that once was ours. Now that the sun scorches and the water lures, I turn in fancy to the gang and speak the magic words, "Say, fellers, who's goin' swimmin'?"

# COMMENTARY

*Water—runoff from abandoned tunnels and from drainage runs, pumped out of the depths of the mines by the huge Cornish pumps, or used to flume the quartz through the mills—accumulated in ponds near most of the mine works. The C and C shaft, jointly used by the California and Consolidated-Virginia mines after the fire, and the pond where Johnny went swimming, were below the eastern border of Chinatown, between N and O streets, and Union and Sutton avenues in Six-Mile Canyon.*

*Further down and to the south, on the crest of a little hummock of a hill rising from the slopes of Mount Davidson, stood the hospital Johnny described, St. Mary Louise, later to include the county hospital of Storey County. The building still stands in lonely solitude, remote from all that Johnny saw, for the Con-Virginia mine works far above near the depot, the C and C shaft 1,400 feet east, and the stamp mills—all have vanished.*

*Hidden in a ravine then as it is today was the Nevada Brewery, which became part of the Virginia City scene in the early sixties. At first, the brewery was built down near Spanish Mill in the Flowery area, but in Johnny's time it was near the C and C shaft. It was operated by Louis Rich, whose drivers delivered beer in shining, brightly painted trucks drawn by proud-stepping Clydesdale horses. For many years the brewery was the home of a mining engineer and his wife, who bought it in 1932 and were said to have found $2,400 in gold in the yard. In 1962 the Subramuniya Yoga Order bought the brewery with the intention of using it as a retreat. The Reverend Mother Christney, a native of Gold Hill, was in charge.*

*St. Mary's Hospital was built in 1876 on six acres of land given to the Sisters of Charity by Mrs. John Mackay in the preceding summer, not long before the Great Fire. The site was known then as Van Bokkelen's Gardens, but the owner, General J. L. Van Bokkelen, had been killed in an explosion in the summer of 1873, and if there had been any gardens on the land, they had shriveled from lack of water in the months that followed.*

*The fund-raising drive to finance the building of the hospital was conducted by Father Patrick Manogue and the Sisters of Charity, who already were teaching parochial schools, one for girls and one for boys, in Virginia City. Contributions came not only from Gold Hill and Virginia City, where the priest and the Sisters sought them, but from as far away as San Francisco.*

*After John Mackay's death many years later, it was said that he had given $500 a month regularly to support the hospital, which often could not have survived without his help. Many of the patients could not afford to pay for their care in the years of borrasca. The miners contributed a dollar a month to the hospital fund. This usually totaled another $500.*

*At the time the hospital was to open in mid-March of 1876, Mrs. James G. Fair gave a "first-class" range with boiler attached, broiler, and facilities for the heating of "smoothing" irons. But all the information that John Mackay would let the papers mention was that he had provided twenty-five dollar cords of wood.*[1]

*According to Dan de Quille, who had just as much sympathy for them as Sam Davis and even more anecdotes, the Piutes did not care for liquor. Hunger was their consuming concern. One rare reference to drinking by a Piute occurred in January 1878, when two Piute braves who had gotten drunk staged a violent battle on the Divide. Captain Bob ordered his henchmen to take them away to their camp, then told the press that "the whiskey that did the mischief" was furnished by the wife of a "one-legged man named Crane." The* Enterprise *sourly added, "For years we have been hearing about the one-legged man in connection with drunken Indians."*[2]

Flanking their side-arm pumper, firemen posed with friends between blazes.

The Corporation firehouse (above) boasted a firebell and observation platform. It was well that it did. The tinderbox potentialities of Virginia City are suggested by the view of C Street (below), taken at the turn of the century.

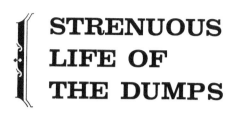

# STRENUOUS
# LIFE OF
# THE DUMPS

Y EARS AGO IN Virginia City, we children made the class line
clear and distinct. If a boy gathered wood on the dumps,
he belonged to the common people, which was my crowd.
If he didn't, he belonged to the tony bunch, or wanted to. In
either event, we looked upon him as altogether too stuck-up
to make good company.

Never was there more interesting society than that which
gathered at the dumps. Boys and girls and men and women
used to dash wildly over the immense heaps of waste rock after
planks, blocks, and miscellaneous bits of wood that had been
dumped out after serving their term of usefulness in the mines.
Most of the rejected wood was wet, some of it soaked through
and almost as heavy as lead, but when dried and cut into lengths
to fit the stove it did fairly well for cooking purposes and was
therefore much in demand. It didn't cost anything in money;
still, we earned every stick that we got. This was because the
wood came out in cars of waste, and its flight down the dump
was accompanied by pieces of rock, some as big as your fist,
some as big as your head. We had to look out for these flying
perils as we scrambled for wood, and more than one kid, myself
included, received honorable wounds in the service.

Between cars we used to sit under the long trestle that ran
out to the dump and play poker or faro for matches. Once when
I was new at the former game, I took a pot with three hearts
and two diamonds, declaring that "all red makes a flush." In-

cidentally, I was bigger than the other players. Later I tried the same thing in an all-aged game and got thrown half way down the dump. Even then, I played in luck. About the time I recovered my balance and sat up to take notice, a car came out and the biggest plank of the day never stopped sliding until it reached a spot where I could put my hand on it without rising. A further evidence of my luck was that not a rock came within three feet of me. It pays to be honest, even when it is compulsory.

Every mining dump had its gang of boys. I lived near the Savage mine and belonged to the Savage gang, of which organization an industrous youngster who was big enough to make me look up to him was the shining light. We called him "Fatty," but if there was ever any disrespect in the designation, it was before I knew him.

According to my usually veracious memory, he ran the dump. Under his direction we dug a tunnel into one of the great weather-packed piles of waste, scooped out a station, and timbered the whole thing in true mining style. During school vacations we almost made a home of that station. After posting a sentinel at the mouth of the tunnel, we would sit inside and play cards or elaborate on neighborhood gossip until we heard the warning shout of "Car! Car!" Then we would all dash pell-mell for the dump. Sometimes a car did not contain even a single stick, and this was sure to make us angry. To our idea the first duty of a mining superintendent was to see that "lots of wood" went over the dump.

While "Fatty's" tunnel was our headquarters, most of the wood came out of the Savage so wet that it oozed water. This meant that it would have to be carefully stacked and left out in the sun for two or three weeks before it was fit for use. Old Peter Nesdale, whose home was beside the dump, had long been doing the drying act and had his yard filled with piles of wood loosely arranged in order to give the sun a chance to do the work expected of it. Some of these piles, ripe for the stove, caught our eye and inspired a cunning scheme. Peter had plenty of dry wood in his cellar; we didn't. Therefore in the black hours of the night while Peter slept, we carried off those several piles for the stove and, stick for stick, replaced them with piles of nice and juicy wood that wouldn't burn if you soaked it in coal oil. "Fatty" made us give Old Peter an honest count, and there isn't any doubt that he had the better of it in weight. What we gave him that night must have weighed at least a ton. Still Peter wasn't satisfied. When he found out what we had done, he stood in his yard and said things that almost made those sodden piles sizzle.

Life along the dumps never lacked excitement. It was a lost day that did not have its fight. Some days had half a dozen. Touching your hand to a piece of wood constituted what we called "tabbing" it, and by the law of the dumps such act made it yours, even though it kept on going and slid far past you. Out of this custom came no end of trouble. In our arithmetic one times one was one, of course, but when the problem became so complicated as to include two "tabs" and only one plank, the result was always a "fight." Even then the victor sometimes lost the prize.

"Pelcher" Williams and "Shamrock" Kelly rushed into a clinch one day, and while they were rolling down the dump, a lean little woman known as "Mrs. Hog" picked up the plank they were fighting over and carried it home. "Pelcher" and "Shamrock" didn't learn of their loss for twenty minutes. In that time they had completed their journey to the bottom of the dump, squared off, and gone at it hammer and tongs until "Pelcher" had concluded that the plank wasn't worth what it was costing him. Meanwhile the rest of us had stood around in a ring and cheered both fighters at once. After "Pelcher" cried quits, we told "Shamrock" how "Mrs. Hog" had once more proved herself worthy of her name. He was mad enough to set her house afire, but he contented himself with turning on "Mrs. Hog's" boy and running him off the dump. That made everything all right. The code of the dump sanctioned vicarious atonement.

Looking back calmly over a score of years I can't say that I think much of the "tabbing" system. It was very fine for the larger boys, but I was one of the "little cusses," and I didn't get all the wood I "tabbed"—not by several cords. Some big

fellows would say, "Go lay down, kid; you missed it a foot."
That settled it. I might as well have missed it a mile for all the
good touching it did me, even though mud from the wood stuck
to my hand as evidence. As for the saying that it is a poor rule
that doesn't work both ways, all I have to remark is that it
worked both ways against me. When I got a plank at the foot
of the dump, a big fellow up near the top would shout, "Drop
it, kid; didn't you see me tab it?" I can still recall how pleasant
that made me feel. It was a great game. I've known one big
fellow to claim more planks out of a single carload than could
have been "tabbed" by a family of acrobats.

# COMMENTARY

*The "tony crowd" up on Bonanza Hill could always buy
wood and coal brought in by the Virginia and Truckee for the
various woodyards, or they could patronize the Chinese peddlers
who trotted about town with two big baskets of wood gleaned from
wherever they were tolerated, each basket swaying at the ends of a
pole balanced on their bent shoulders.*

*But there was not enough money in the paychecks of most miners
to pay for the wood so constantly needed. The little frame cottages,
by no means weatherproof, were lined with muslin which shivered
and undulated with every draft. Filled with children of all ages
from infancy to teens, they required fires every afternoon when the
long chill set in as the sun made its early disappearance behind the
great bulk of Mount Davidson. Wood also was needed for cooking
the hearty meals devoured by the hard-working miners and their
lively children. The family woodpile was constantly diminishing
and constantly growing, as wood hunting became the perennial
chore after school and on Saturdays.*

*The wood dumped out with the waste rock of the mines was a never-ending source. One mine alone, the Con-Virginia, used five hundred thousand feet of lumber in one month to replenish the intricate checkerboard Deidesheimer timbering which lined the drifts, tunnels, and winzes and protected the miners from cave-ins.*

*Scrounging for wood on the dumps was a way of life. John Debo Galloway, a miner's son, later famous as a civil engineer and railroad historian, recalled clambering over the C and C dump northeast of the Catholic church for candle boxes and timbers.[1] The famous Michelson family lived near the Con-Virginia dump before they moved up on the hill near the Andes Mine. They surely visited both dumps in search of wood, for there were many Michelsons, all as industrious as they were brilliant.[2]*

*The Savage dump, where Johnny conducted his wood collecting, was the largest on the Comstock. It and the nearby Hale and Norcross were mountainous mole hills of waste rock and debris, growing ever higher as the miners below cut their way through the rock and clay in quest of another bonanza. Both were deep mines, going down for more than half a mile.*

*The business of combing the dumps was by no means a safe one, and death "tabbed" wood gatherers more than once, as timber and rock plummeted from cars on the trestles above the unwary. In the late seventies a boy hunting wood on the C and C dump stepped on a Giant powder cap and was horribly mangled.[3] A man was found dead one morning near a trestle, his head crushed by a scantling. It was the habit of many men and women to go out to the dumps during the hours between two and three in the morning because it was said that the best wood came out at that time. There seemed some doubt as to how the man died, whether he had been hit by wood falling from the trestle or had had it swung on him in a battle over what Johnny knew as "tabbing."[4]*

*The lumberyard of Breed and Crosby, near the Hale and Norcross dump and the Savage Switch, was another favorite with the junior wood collectors. Sent there to pick up chips and odd portable pieces of wood, they often lingered to play around the loading platform. One of Johnny's contemporaries in the seventies, little eight-year-old Johnny O'Keefe, tried to leap from the platform to the second car in a string of moving flat cars, missed and fell under the wheels.[5] Another time dump cars loaded with waste rock got away from the train on the C and C side tracks, headed out of control for the dump and ready collision with whatever stood in the way. The collision was with standing box cars, and it was violent.*[6]

*The life of a gang member was never a peaceful one. They fought among themselves, and they were intolerant of newcomers as well as those who dared to be different. When Ensign Albert A. Michelson, U.S.N., instructor in physics and chemistry at the United States Naval Academy at Annapolis, came home on leave by way of the "lightning express" on the Virginia and Truckee in September of 1878, he took his younger sister, Miriam, to the store to buy a pail of ice cream for the family. He wore his splendid uniform, complete with sword. His head was bare and his black hair shone with pomade.*

*It was more than the Con-Virginia gang could tolerate. Such a sight in their area, which surrounded the Michelson home, was a taunt and an affront to their existence. Albert handed his sword to Miriam and laid about him mightily with the ice cream bucket, which soon lost its lid. He beat off the attackers, but not until the scene was prophetic of a Keystone comedy.*[7] *Michelson would soon measure the speed of light and go on to a career that in 1907 would win him the first Nobel prize to be awarded an American. Miriam grew up to become a popular novelist and a sister-in-law of the Arthur McEwen who had crusaded against the Virginia and Truckee Railroad in 1879–1881.*

*Denis Mahoney, author of* The Great Comstock Lode from 1859 to 1937, *recalled the fistfights among rival gangs, the challenges and defiances concerning chips on shoulders and toes on lines: "Every street and mine had a boy champion, and boys, like American Navy sailors, always traveled about town in groups for the same reason as sailors do in foreign ports."*[8]

Virginia City, in keeping with the tradition of western mining towns, had a sizeable Chinese subculture. Some aspects of their life in the metropolis of Washoe were sketched by an artist for *Harper's Weekly*.

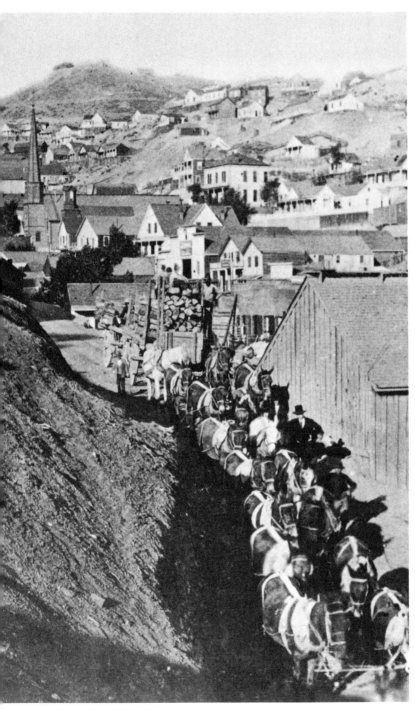

Lack of wood was a continuing problem in the Comstock with its
treeless hills. "The demand was so great that several hundred
laborers were constantly employed in cutting and hauling firewood,"
wrote Eliot Lord.

# HO, FOR TREADWAY'S!

IT TAKES A MINING CAMP to get the full measure of joy out of a picnic. You who have great parks almost at your doors can't imagine what a picnic means to the small boy who is surrounded by sagebrush. I was that kind of a small boy, and I know. In Virginia City we looked on picnic days as second in importance only to such days as Christmas and the Fourth of July and circus days. If there was even a slight chance of going, we drew heavily on the bank of anticipation, and then if we were disappointed, we were bankrupt indeed.

One great feature of those picnics in the golden days was the opportunity it gave us to partake of that notorious forbidden fruit known as the green apple. Whenever we read in the paper or saw on the billboards a flaring advertisement that started off, "Ho, for Treadway's!" we realized anew that life had much in store for us.

Treadway's was the picnic park down in Carson, and as it was thirty-two miles away by the crooked Virginia and Truckee Railroad, a bully ride would come before and follow after the feast of green apples. Then there was the falling into the pond with your clothes on, and the target-shooting, and the foot-races, and the trips to town to see what you could see. Surely this was a program of the kind that the small boy would have thought out and suggested, if he had been given the opportunity.

Cynical grown-ups used to say that picnics were all alike.

That was all for effect. I had been to Sabbath-school jubilations, and I had seen the Emmet Guard stack arms and help themselves to a good time. Therefore, no peddler of second-hand philosophy could convince me that they were quite the same. If he had said something intelligent, such as, "A poor picnic is better than none," I might have agreed with him.

The great picnic of the year was given by the Miners' Union. What a time that used to be! Families that sent no representative to Carson that day insured themselves against being on speaking terms with their neighbors. Only one of three things could keep one in town. If it wasn't force of circumstance, it was lack of intelligence; if it wasn't either of those, it was a desire to make way with unguarded valuables. Force of circumstances got me once or twice, but there is one particular time that it didn't. I mention this particular time because it brought about my progression from playing faro for matches to putting real money down on the red and black.

For many weeks before the picnic, I had been doing business with the junk man. After I had sold all the white glass, bits of brass and copper, and old iron that I could pick up, I turned my attention to rags, which commodity was bringing half a cent a pound. This seemed a fair price, and but for unexpected interference I might, in my enthusiasm, have denuded our house of all clothing not in immediate use. Despite obstacles, I did fairly well, and the morning of the picnic found me with $2.75 knotted tightly in the corner of a handkerchief. I was rich—and greedy. I didn't want to pay my way to the grounds and back.

A few passenger coaches and a long string of flat cars, fenced around and provided with seats, made up the picnic train, or, rather the first section; for the great crowd got away in installments that day. I slipped away from my big sisters, knowing that they would make me pay fare, and got in with a gang of kids who couldn't have paid if they wanted to. As the train was running through town and every mine whistle in the camp was screeching "Goodbye!" I was looking for a place to hide. That was easy. When the conductor passed by I was under a seat. So was the rest of the gang.

At last we reached Treadway's, which I am beginning to suspect was a poor excuse for a park, but that is now. It looked like heaven then. After eating four green apples and three green pears, I hurried over to the pond, jumped on a raft, took a ride, upset the raft, and got wet enough to attract everybody's attention. The sun warmed up to his work and dried me in two hours. Afterwards I was sorry he hurried so.

No sooner was I dry than I followed the crowd to where a big man in his shirt sleeves gave a pretty wheel a twirl and shouted, "Round she goes! Where she stops nobody knows!" Occasionally he added, "Even money on the red and black; six to one on the green. Step up, gentlemen. Here's a chance to make your expenses."

I still had all of my $2.75, and the expense argument couldn't have appealed to me, but when I saw a man in front of me win four straight times on the red, I tremblingly dropped a quarter of a dollar on the black. The black won; I "pinched" a quarter; it won again; I "pinched" another quarter; another win and another "pinch." I was six bits ahead! Like the greenhorn in the story, I wanted to know right away how long that sort of a thing had been going on. I kept on trembling and betting, and "pinching"—sometimes. At one time I had hopes of winning the bankroll. It was when I was $1.75 to the good.

Pride trips over its own feet. What got me going the wrong way was sticking to the red. After it had lost nine straight times I concluded that warm colors were not for me. My money went on the somber, and then the gay had a run of luck. My heart sank with my pile. When I reached the lone quarter stage, I had one of those cold chills. I held that quarter in my hand and watched the red win twelve times running. Then I put my quarter on the black. The green won!

One of my big sisters gave me money enough to buy dinner, but, alas! nothing for ice cream, or soda, or popcorn, or peanuts, or cigarettes. The only thing I got besides dinner money was a real saucy lecture about gambling. All I can remember of it now is that she spoke of "big thieves" and "little fools." I didn't even answer her back. I was too miserable.

That wasn't a good afternoon. Something was the matter

with the baseball game, and the target-shooting, and the foot races. Nobody seemed to know how to do anything right. From every place on the grounds I could hear an awful voice shouting, "Round she goes!" I kept figuring up what that $2.75 would have got me. I even regretted that I had not bought a ticket for the picnic, instead of smuggling my way. My conscience was thoroughly aroused.

On the way home I didn't try to hide, but somehow the conductor overlooked me. There was my luck coming back to me, and me broke! A minute later the easiest member of all the gang wanted to match me for a quarter. That's always the way.

# COMMENTARY

*Johnny had to raise the price of his ticket to Treadway's because his father believed in a boy's learning to provide for his own pleasures. Children who were really unable to raise the money for this excursion were often provided for by kindly men of Gold Hill and Virginia City. The price of the round trip and admission to Treadway's was $2.50. For those who drove down by horse and carriage, admission to the grounds was $1.00. By the time Johnny was nine or ten, there were several younger children in the Waldorf family, and a third was on the way in the summer of 1881. His mother was looking for peace rather than picnics. Obviously, his father could not give up a day's pay for a day at Treadway's. So Johnny was left to the somewhat casual supervision of his two older sisters.*

*Picnic trains were made up of old passenger cars, flatcars, and occasionally boxcars without seats. The flatcars were fitted with benches and fenced around the top to prevent adventurous small boys from taking headers over the sides. The number of cars reserved varied from twenty to twenty-one, apparently about all that were on hand for summer excursions. Preparations were begun well ahead of time, with a "master of transportation up from Carson City" to make sure that no traffic snarls interfered with the regular business of the railroad. Two engines were required to pull the long train of cars on its way to Carson City and Treadway's.*

*Each flatcar accommodated 150 visible riders, and such stowaways as Johnny and his friends were no novelty. The public school picnic on Saturday, June 8, 1878, was distinguished for the fact that "only five attempted to steal a ride."[1] At least only five were discovered. It seems to have been a status symbol to be a successful stowaway.*

*Departure of the picnic trains was usually at 8 A.M., but long before that hour crowds of children loud with excitement were racing up and down the depot platform, dancing and whirling—and in the case of the boys, scuffling. The girls were in brightly colored cottons with flying ribbons, the boys scrubbed and polished, full of threats as to what they intended to do when they reached Treadway's. The adults, especially the young men, were no less excited, many of them having dashed into the already open doors of clothing stores along C Street to buy new linen dusters and straw hats on their way to the depot. The astute proprietors of such stores often opened them as early as seven o'clock on a picnic day, which was usually a Saturday.*

*Picnic trains invariably got off on time. Excitement mounted as the busy and very important master of transportation and the conductors completed their surveys and assembled to give the signal for the start. Usually, the engineers at the throttles were known to all and named in the newspaper stories. So were the engines.*

*The highest pitch of anticipation was reached when the two engines and the cars, one after another, were gobbled up by the E Street tunnel, to the screams, shouts, and whistles of the passengers. Smoke, cinders, soot, heat, and darkness made no difference. Once into the first tunnel they were on their way!*

*It took about fifteen minutes of darting into the darkness of tunnels and then out to bright flashes of sage, houses, and mine works, before the train reached Gold Hill. The last tunnel was that under old Fort Homestead. When the picnic train emerged from that tunnel, the Virginia City delegation could see the Gold Hill* crowds milling around the depot on the far side of the canyon. Eight or ten carloads could be depended on to be added at Gold Hill, and there were times when hundreds of youngsters were left forlorn and deserted on the depot platform.

Mrs. Bowers, the Washoe seeress, accompanied the picnickers on the public school picnic of 1878. A rumor had gotten around during the week before that she had prophesied the collapse of the Crown Point Trestle as the train passed over it. She scotched the "great scare" by blandly trusting herself to the Virginia and Truckee. Rounding the Gold Hill depot, the excursion train crept through a cut in the wall of Gold Canyon and approached the Crown Point Trestle. Spanning the ravine where the Crown Point mine works lay, the trestle was 350 feet long and 90 feet high, though it must have looked far longer and higher to all on board that day. But it proved to be as strong as Mrs. Bowers' faith, and the train went on its winding way.

At the Silver City switch, below the 600-foot-long tunnel at American Flat, longest on the line, more picnickers would be waiting. In fact, additional recruits came aboard at the Belcher, Scales, Mound House, and Empire, the little engines straining and dragging hard on the load as the train got heavier and longer.

Whether it was a Miners' Union picnic or a public school picnic, the ride into Carson City was to a rising pandemonium of exultation, for then it was only a mile more to Farmer Treadway's. The ranch lay to the west of town, and the train ran along the boundary of the grounds as the tracks headed north towards Bowers' Mansion, Ophir, Steamboat, Huffaker's, and Reno.

Farmer Treadway was in his sixties by the time Johnny was old enough to go to picnics. But the famous farmer always made a point of driving from his home at the corner of Washington and Elizabeth in downtown Carson City when a picnic train was due from Virginia City. There he would be waiting at the ranch gate to greet the thousands as they surged into the grounds.

Aaron D. Treadway liked being known as "Farmer Treadway," but his career had been anything but bucolic. A Connecticut Yankee, brick mason, and Mexican War veteran, he had joined the California gold rush when he was thirty-four and within ten years had tried his fortune in one way or another at Weaverville, Sutter's

*Mill, and Sacramento. He settled at Carson City shortly after the
Comstock rush in 1859; there he farmed, served in the Nevada
territorial legislature, and sent the first load of potatoes and beets
on the Virginia and Truckee to Virginia City when the railroad
began running between the two towns. The ranch was big and included not only the orchard where Johnny sampled green apples
but many shade trees, wide expanses of lawns, a grape arbor, and
a loghouse spring.*

*At most picnics, including those of the Miners' Union, there
were target matches, archery contests for the ladies and races for
men, boys, and girls. The prizes were often quite elaborate. Groups
of young ladies often walked the mile into town where the superintendent of the Mint and his staff were happy to act as guides.
There was also the big stone capitol and other public buildings to
be visited. Boys like Johnny either yielded to the blandishments of
concessionaires or relaxed on the lawns. It was considered something to boast about, however, when the* Enterprise *could report that
there was "no drunkenness, fighting or other trouble to mar the
general festivities."²*

*Departure from Treadway's was set for 4:30 P.M. as a rule,
with those in charge rounding up the kids at four. It took nearly
three hours for the train to make its way back up the twisting,
snakelike grade to Virginia City. Even with the three engines required for the homeward journey, the train strained and labored
up the grade, the engines often seeming about to nip the last car in
the train as it trailed around a loop that all but tied itself in a knot.
One after another, the cars were dropped off at the various stops
where blithe passengers had waited so impatiently in the morning.
One by one, the tunnels were entered, and one after another the
mine whistles welcomed the picnickers back to the mountain.*

*Because the sun disappears early behind the great shoulders of
Mount Davidson, even in summer, picnic trains always returned
into blue twilight and a sombre, almost mournful world. It was
often as late as seven and the kids dispersed quickly, some to relate
great adventures and discoveries, some, like the chastened Johnny,
to say nothing whatever.*

In San Francisco, the "interest in speculation" was especially active as indicated by this sketch by L. Henry.

# TAKING
# A CHANCE

IN MY DAY on the Comstock almost everbody took an active interest in some kind of speculation. The babies were barred, of course, but I've seen infants making a faro chip do duty as a teething ring. We small boys went further and played cards for matches. Sometimes we got blooded and bet such treasures as tops and marbles. One budding plunger wagered his hat and went home bareheaded, but I shall not mention his name because his father robbed him of fame by retrieving the hat and incidentally bringing about the "lammin'" of the winner for gambling.

Our dads wanted to do all the gambling themselves. The stronger the game, the better they liked it, and they all seemed to be inspired by the prehistoric gambler who said, "Money won't grow in your hand." Still, this was to be expected. They risked their lives every time they went to work, and when a man gambles with what God gave him, he isn't apt to hesitate over staking what he has picked up for himself.

The favorite game with our fathers was stocks. We little fellows didn't understand it, but we thought it would be made plain when we grew up. Since then we've come to the conclusion we never will be old enough to master it. I got my wisdom free of cost, but some of my friends paid dearly for theirs. It is still as much of a mystery to me as it was in the days when the sight of a crowd around a stock board filled us with contempt. I remember the first crowd of that kind that I ever ran into. One

130

of the neighbor's boys was with me. He burrowed his way through a jam of excited men, but soon came back to me snorting with disgust. "Aw," he said, "I thought it was a fight!"

How anybody could become interested in a game where you couldn't watch the dealer was beyond our powers of comprehension, but Virginia City was like every other place. The grown-up folks didn't believe that wisdom could come from the mouths of babes. Women as well as men put their all in stocks. When the newspaper came flying over the fence or banged against the front door, they seized it and turned hastily to the market page. Though the front page told of the death of the nation's greatest statesman or the blowing up of a czar, it made no difference. They paid no attention to the news until they had looked over the stock quotations.

If their eyes were weak, they would get the children to read to them. One kind-hearted lady used to call to me almost every day, "Johnny, come over like a good boy and tell me what's in the paper." I knew what that meant. She wanted to know about stocks. Many a day on her account I missed precious opportunities to have fun, but I'm entitled to no credit for that. It was her pies and cakes that lured me.

I would sit in her kitchen half an hour at a time reading such jargon as "Andes, 25 cents bid, 27 cents asked"; or "Bullion, opened 42, closed $41\frac{3}{4}$"; going through the long list, following it up with the sales, and closing the recital with mining news about dips, spurs, angles, winzes, up-raises, cross-cuts, inclines, and what not. The dear lady understood it all, but my expert knowledge was confined to pie and cake. Her stock of these commodities was always of superior quality, but the demand always exceeded the visible supply. If I had posted a board, it would often have read: "Cake opened strong, and all offerings found ready takers. Pie, one piece bid: two pieces asked. Extension work at the mouth of the shaft may become necessary in the near future."

I didn't need to go to the neighbors to hear stock talk. Dad got the fever soon after he struck the camp. Mother used to say to me, "Some day we're going back East," but for years none of the stocks in which Dad invested showed any disposition to furnish us with the price of transportation. All the while I was throwing out my little chest and informing every small boy I met that "we" were going back East.

Finally, "our" Ophir took a boom. Dad's holdings rose in value to $10,000 and mother began to talk of buying a farm. I was a real king, as far as feelings went. The stock kept going upward. Dad was worth $15,000 for at least a minute. He wanted $20,000, the clock ticked a few times; the bottom fell out of Ophir, and Mother's dream farm fell with it, for Dad was broke. The next day a kid across the street yelled to me, "You ain't so stuck up now. Goin' back East! Maybe you're goin' to Gold Hill." That was kind! From where we lived, it was almost a mile to Gold Hill.

Everybody had a hard luck story. Some had their goods packed when the crash came. I knew little fellows who got no Christmas presents because their dad had to pay an assessment on Confidence or Justice or some other mine with a sarcastic name. My dad never let the fever get that kind of a hold on him. He would sooner lose part of his stock than ignore Christmas. At least once a year he made me so happy that I forgot all about back East and the terrible day when Ophir wrecked our hopes.

Speaking of Ophir, "Old Doc," a neighborhood celebrity, used to say: "She reminds me of an old woman I knew in Missouri. This woman used to sit suckin' a gin bottle. When she started in, all she owned was a little patch of ground with a cabin on it, but with every drink she kept growin' richer and richer, and about the time she had the bottle straight up in the air she owned the whole state of Missouri. Then without any warnin' she'd slide unter the table, and that ended the performance. You don't catch me buying' any Ophir!"

Some people had better luck than we. A few made their pile and went away. This helped the game, for those who stayed behind took hope and decided not to break themselves of the habit of carrying a few gold pieces to the broker's office every payday. Many a man delved in the depths year after year, earning his bread in more sweat than the prophets ever dreamed of, and got nothing out of his wage save board and lodgings.

Some of these unfortunates economized to buy a few more shares of stock or to pay assessments on what they had.

What a nightmare those assessments were! The young felt them as well as the old, even though small boys were barred from the game. A father might be fond of his offspring, but the constant levying of assessments on his stock didn't improve his patience with a child who got noisy while he was studying the quotations in the paper. No doubt many a "lammin' " that was administered down in our neighborhood had its inception in a meeting of mining magnates. I remember at least one youngster who was wise in his generation. I saw him come dashing out the front door of his home with the toe of his dad's boot pursuing him closely. When he reached me he took a long breath and said: "Gee, I wish Kentuck would declare a dividend."

# COMMENTARY

*Dealing in stocks, frequently buying on a margin and always in peril, miners gambled their hopes instead of banking what was left of their paychecks after the bills were paid. Not only did they crowd around the bulletin boards of the brokers on C Street when they were on the surface, but as soon as the wires came up from the San Francisco Stock Exchange, the news of how the stocks were faring was sent down to the big rooms in the depths where the men rested between bouts with heat and hard rock.*

*A few men among the miners laid by substantial sums, but most of them lost far more than they made. One miner confided to his diary that he had lost $300 out of $800 in stocks in a period of ten days in the late seventies.[1]*

*The wily operators down in the San Francisco Stock Exchange, the men who speculated with plenty of capital behind them, often cleverly manipulated the market into all sorts of acrobatics. It was*

*a rich man's game. They were too fast for the miners, too fast for
many of their associates on the exchange. The miners thought that
all a man needed to speculate successfully was knowledge of the
rock itself, but in time they learned how wrong they were. Eliot
Lord said they kept on speculating even after they knew what they
were up against.*

*Johnny must have been twelve or thirteen years old when stocks
were as low as those quotations he read to the neighboring pie and
cake expert, for in 1880 began the long slide to oblivion. Old timers
might dig into old tunnels and shafts, a mine might muddle on with
crews of eight or ten men, but the glory of the Comstock passed with
the eighties.*

*The Ophir was quite probably the mine where Jacob Waldorf
first worked when he arrived in Virginia City in May 1871. It was
a favorite with everybody—miners, operators, speculators. Joseph
L. King, author of* A History of the San Francisco Stock Exchange, *recalled Ophir with nostalgia and tenderness. "In olden
times," he said, "an Ophir deal rejoiced the hearts of all."*[2] *When
Ophir's stock rose, so did stock of all the mines along the Lode and
even down towards the Flowery Range.*

*There was a sharp rise in Ophir in November 1877, and every-
thing about that excitement tallies with Johnny's recollections of the
time they almost made enough money to go back East in glory.
Twenty thousand dollars would have made them a well-to-do farming family in southern Michigan.*

*There is no doubt but what something was found at the 1,900-foot
level of the Ophir in early November 1877, when Johnny was seven
years old. News leaked out, and rumors went like hot zephyrs
through the town. Nobody knew anything and some believed everything. The Ophir was always bothered by subterranean water,
which could come spurting out of the rock itself when a pick cut
into a stream. So when management announced that it would be
necessary to delay long enough to build a bulkhead in case of water,
stockholders accepted the explanation. They were promised admit-
tance to the 1,900-foot level as soon as it was secure. Then they
could examine the rock and make their own judgments. All were
assured that it was a strike of importance. "Right royally Ophir
rode to the top, passing the bonanza with the same feeling of superi-*

*ority as she flitted by wild cats," reported the San Francisco* Alta *on November 9, 1877, adding that "Reports were plentiful that certain brokers were short and consequently in a fit condition to be cinched."[3]*

*This was where Jacob D. Waldorf was vulnerable. "The short in some cases made desperate efforts to make cover," said the* Alta. *"They were headed off from breaking the stock, and this was the game of those manipulating the stock the balance of the afternoon."*

*For two days Ophir was "bounding and rebounding." Monday, November 9, according to the* Alta, *had turned out to be the most exciting day of the year. Everything had "wanted to advance." In fact the writer feared that unless some check "had been put on the rising prices, they would have reached the most exaggerated figures."*

*In an informal, expansive deal in the Palace Hotel on Saturday, November 10, two hundred and fifty shares of Ophir had exchanged hands at $57 a share, but when business closed on Monday, November 12, the shares were at thirty-five dollars. It was as high as they went, before the Ophir began to slide.*

*Since much of Jacob Waldorf's Ophir stock was held on a margin, his broker undoubtedly cried for "mud," and the order from Virginia City came too late. There is a story in the family that Jacob Waldorf, not satisfied with the telegraph or the way his broker was handling the business, went down to San Francisco to see him. Whether or not he took such an active part in the frantic boom, he was helpless in the outcome. There was no trip back East, no farm, no release from daily toil in a dark, hot mine.*

*The boom in Ophir had not impressed the* Alta, *which had tartly commented on the fact that the half-dozen miners working in shifts on the 1,900-foot level of the Ophir were not permitted to talk with outsiders and were kept in the foreman's changing room with a "guard of honor," even though they were fed on "the fat of the land." This was an old dodge with Comstock mines and one Ophir had practiced more aggressively in the past.*

*"We have cautioned our readers about trusting the stock either way," growled the* Alta. *"There was too much mystery connected with the manipulation, and the story was that a large number of shorts were out and a thousand and one stories circulated, all having a favorable tendency to the lifting of the stock."[4]*

*By late November, Ophir was so secretive that a door had been put across the 1,900-foot drift and a padlock fastened to it. The deal had an unpleasant odor to the* Alta, *which prophesied that the public stockholders wouldn't have a chance until "the insiders are loaded up with stock if the development is good or sold out and heavily short if of small amount."*

*A similar sort of boom lifted Sierra Nevada in the late summer of the following year. All during the late seventies when no new bonanza followed that in the Con-Virginia and California, mine managements made efforts to keep up enthusiasm, sustain and buoy the hopes of stockholders. Savage made a great show of building stairs from C Street down to the mine office on D Street in August 1878 and bulkheaded a sidewalk built along the mine property where it fronted on C so that it "looked like a rope walk." The* Enterprise *coyly wondered if they were preparing to "fence a bonanza."[5] But nothing came of it.*

*However, just a few weeks later, big excitement centered around the Sierra Nevada, far up the line to the north. Stockholders were permitted to examine the ore on the 2,100-foot level, and stocks were "rampant." Every mine on the north boomed like a rocket. The Mexican, the Alta, the Lady Bryan, and the Wells Fargo in the northeast part of town rose with Sierra Nevada. The town was in such a state of jubilation that almost everybody joined the evening promenade along C Street the night of August 28, 1878, and an* Enterprise *reporter wrote that "it is beginning again to look like old times."[6]*

*The next day stockholders were admitted to the Sierra Nevada, the Ophir, and the Julia. Miners took samples of likely ore to the assayer. But by December 1 all was quiet. No one was being admitted to the mines unless he could prove he had the "requisite amount of stock." Two weeks later, a man named Duncan McKay sued Western Union for $2,149.87—an amount he insisted he had lost in a stock sale because his wire ordering the sale of 250 shares of Mexican had not reached Thomas Bell, his San Francisco broker, until too late to make the maximum profit.[7] At that, he was better off than Jacob D. Waldorf had been in November 1877.*

*By December 28, 1878, there was no doubt about it: the bottom had fallen out of Sierra Nevada, and it was being referred to as "a* deal." *It was this Sierra Nevada deal, according to Grant H. Smith, which killed the hopes and broke the hearts of the people of the Comstock.*[8] *Everybody but the manipulators lost heavily in this fiasco, San Francisco stockholders as well as those on the Comstock. Miriam Michelson, the novelist, was bitter about it and blamed "knaves" in Virginia City for sending out stories of strikes that were never made, new discoveries that bore no promise, and accounts of sales that never happened. But she also blamed the "fools" in San Francisco for swallowing the yarns.*

*Many men made fortunes on the Comstock, but many, many more did not. The eighties were bitter years for the miners. Work was not steady, and the future of their sons was bleak, for even prospects of becoming an engine wiper or a pick boy had faded. No wonder many a young fellow went down the Geiger Grade or through Devil's Gate in search of hope and the great adventure somewhere else.*

Weighing the load at the Gould and Curry Mine, 1865.

The "extraordinary" Gould & Curry mill looked to Lord like "the mansion of some wealthy landowner rather than a mill built in a barren district to crush silver ore"—except for the "impertinent clatter of the stamps."

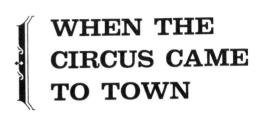

# WHEN THE CIRCUS CAME TO TOWN

I CAN REMEMBER WHEN I was not only willing but eager and anxious to get up at two o'clock in the morning. This abnormal state of mind took hold of me once a year and lasted one consecutive day. The very next morning I would require at least three calls and the threat of a "dose of strap oil" to make me crawl out from under the covers.

What do you suppose made the wonderful difference? No, not Christmas. In our house the room with the Christmas tree in it didn't open for business before six o'clock. What used to get the rise out of me was something better than candy and presents. It was the coming of the circus. We Virginia City kids didn't want to miss anything. With us the circus began with the arrival of the wonderful canvas-covered trains and the unloading of the animals. The boy who was denied this pleasure was the object of mingled pity and contempt, and we used to say of him, "Aw, he might as well be a girl."

For weeks before the circus came to town, I made daily trips from the Geiger Grade to the Divide, taking in all the billboards. On the eve of the great event I climbed into bed with a last touching appeal, "Ma, don't forget to call me." Mother was more reliable than any alarm clock ever invented, but this didn't keep me from dreaming that she had overslept herself and that the cases containing the "lines and taggers" were all inside the tents when I got down to Alexander's lot. That was an awful dream, and how glad I was when I heard Mother say,

"Johnny, get up," and opened my eyes to find it wasn't true. In five minutes I was up, almost dressed and out in the street, finishing my dressing on the way to the old depot, where the circus trains unloaded.

Half a dozen or more boys were there before me. Dozens and dozens came on the run after I arrived, until fifty of us stood around blowing on our hands in an effort to keep warm. How the time dragged! "Mebbe she's wrecked," suggested a skinny little parvenue from up the hill, and we all shuddered. It was a horrible thought. "Reddy" Kelly braced up and said defiantly, "Bet you she ain't," and then we all felt better.

We froze some more. A whistle sounded far away, and we were warm in a second. "Here she comes!" Everybody shouted at once. She whistled again, and my heart beat faster. By the time the first section rolled up to the platform I was so happy I wouldn't have changed places with a bonanza king.

We speculated on the contents of the cages. Unsightly canvas hid the pictures and the names, but size and shape could not be concealed. "Bet they've got the old hippopotamus in there."

"That's the giraffe's cage."

"Hey, Billy, here's the lion's cage."

"Naw, that ain't it."

"Bet it is. Didn't I hear him roar?"

We spent hours of joy watching the circus hands transferring that precious freight to the platform. We looked over the horses with a critical eye and chose the ones that pleased us most. It didn't matter that we got no bill of sale. They were ours for the moment. We followed the last of the cages down to the circus grounds and watched the tents go up before we remembered that we hadn't had any breakfast, and we wouldn't have thought of it then if the circus cooks hadn't begun to get busy with pots and pans. Then we ran home, bolted down a few bites and a cup of coffee, grabbed a "hunk" of bread in each hand, smeared the bread with jelly, and did the rest of our break-fasting as we ran back to the circus grounds. That was the annual experience.

As for the performance itself, some of us saw it and some of us didn't. I was invariably one of the favored. In eleven years, beginning with the time when I saw Nellie Brown juggle knives while she rode two horses "going at a maddening speed" until old John Robinson almost made me cross-eyed with his two rings, I missed just one circus. I shall always believe that one was the best circus that ever came west.

We lived in sight of the "city of tents," and all afternoon and all evening I was imprisoned in the back yard. Clinging to the fence, I saw the people going to the circus. There seemed to be millions of them. And a third of them were boys! Fate had singled me out for punishment. I looked and yearned and cried. Did I say cried? Bawled would be better. One of my sisters advised me to be careful lest my tears wash the fence away. Truly, it was the dampest day I ever spent.

Aside from my failure to see that one wonderful circus, I have something to regret. I never carried water to the elephant. There was a neighbor's boy who achieved even greater distinction. One circus day before the menagerie tent was ready for its attractions, he began a minute inspection of the cages that were scattered about the grounds. He got along nicely for a time, peeking in at the lion and the tiger from the front grating near the driver's seat, and even catching sight of some strange beast that was new to him. In the course of his investigations he came upon the leopard's cage. He learned the identity of the occupant afterward. No beast came to the bars at first, and he carelessly put his hand where it could be reached.

Nine cats all clawing at once couldn't have given him the mark that he got from that leopard. His screams sounded above the roar of the lion. If he hadn't made such an awful noise, he would have been a hero. As it was we paid him deference until another boy almost had his head kicked off and a few weeks later came among us wearing a silver plate under his hair.

I never "nipped" under the canvas but once. That was when a little road show called the Great Arabian Circus came to town. It had only one tent, and the gang agreed that no self-respecting boy could think of paying. Eleven of us went under the canvas in eleven seconds. It wasn't worth the trouble. "Shark" Conlon wanted to bet that he could beat the "world renowed Lorena" riding, and none of us would take him up though we knew that "Shark" wasn't any wonder. There were no elephants and no "lines and taggers," and even the pink lemonade looked sick. We sat on unplaned boards and made fun of the show until a big, ugly fellow threatened to put us out. "Shark" got brave and told him we would be glad to go if he would give us our money back. The big fellow hurried off, but he didn't come back, and we stayed until it was all over. Say, even the clown was bad, but as the philosopher of the gang remarked, "That's what you get for nippin' in under the canvas."

# COMMENTARY

*Virginia City was a great circus town. Everybody loved the circus, from the small boys to the Piute Indians. The two weeks between the arrival of the circus advertising car and the first toot of the engines coming out of the Fort Homestead Tunnel were weeks of anticipation and art appreciation.*

*The small boys were not alone in their admiration of circus advertising art, for the Piutes sauntered reverently along the streets of town, studying every lurid billboard. But the Piute was more literal in his appreciation of the posters. One year there was trouble when a lion and rhinoceros failed to meet in mortal combat as the posters had promised. The Piutes were cheated and furious. An enraged tribesman left the show and began tearing one of the brilliant posters to shreds as he shouted, "Him heap damn lie!" As an* Enterprise *reporter put it, "The red men are all great admirers of horse opera."[1]*

*The circus lot was down at the foot of Washington Street, and the tents were raised in one of the fields owned by Louis and John Alexander, proprietors of the Virginia Milk Dairy. When the circus train pulled into town it did not enter the last tunnel but stopped at the old depot near the Gould and Curry Works. From*

*there the big wagons and trucks were hauled to Washington Street
and then down east to the circus lot.*

*The year after Adam Forepaugh first put the circus on rails, he
came to Virginia City. That was in May 1878. His circus had
become a huge affair with "Golden Chariots," "Tableau Cars,"
and "Palace Dens" for the performing animals. The brilliant
posters studied by small boys and Piutes that year promised a
two-thousand-dollar male hippopotamus, performing elephants,
Arctic Ocean sea lions, polar bears, the baby elephant "Chicago,"
a six-ton rhinocerus, and 1,500 rare wild animals.*

*There were to be six famous clowns, but probably not Dan Rice,
the most famous clown of all. Dan had been with Forepaugh for
years, but he had a drinking problem, and in 1878 he took the
pledge. At the time Forepaugh's circus first wound up the grade to
Virginia City, Dan was on the temperance lecture circuit; there
were some who suspected that there was more often gin than water
in the pitcher from which the speaker refreshed himself.*[2]

*Forepaugh's advertising in 1878 made much of the fine condition
and high spirits of his horses. He reminded all that his horses no
longer had to drag heavy wagons from town to town over rough and
muddy roads; therefore, they were not tired and worn out when
they arrived for a performance. So Johnny and his pals had reason
to admire the sleek beauties, among which were horses that Young
Melville, the Apollo Horseman of America, would ride.*

*Adam Forepaugh was forty-seven when he arrived in Virginia
City in 1878, with a red face and wind-blown side whiskers. He
had become so powerful in the circus world that even Barnum was
about to agree to peaceful co-existence. They would soon sign an
agreement to keep out of the same towns, but it was not kept very
long. Forepaugh, who had begun life in Philadelphia and who had
learned butchering in his father's shop, often went into the cook
tent of his circus to see that the meat was properly cut. He frequently sat out under canvas in front, holding court on opening
day, looking enough like his advertisements to be easily recognized.
People who came out of the tent for the menagerie and prepared to
enter the Big Top were often welcomed by the great man himself.*[3]

*The Great Arabian Circus played Virginia City in 1879 and
the reporter for the Virginia City* Chronicle *didn't think any more*

*of it than Johnny did. But it was not all bad. There was a balloon ascension, a man with an "iron jaw," and trick horses. The reporter thought the performing steeds were San Francisco hack horses "who had to lean against each other to stand up."⁴ But he was positive the two-hundred-pound anvils which the man with the iron jaw flung about the ring with his teeth looked solid enough to be the real thing. As a finale, the iron-jawed man gripped his teeth on a leather band from which dangled a five-hundred-pound brass cannon. While he swung by his feet, the cannon was fired, and the* Chronicle *reporter opined that "He should be secured to deliver the Fourth of July oration in Carson."*

*The balloon ascension was a teaser for the main performance. It cost the town nothing and was attended by everyone who was above ground. The big bag was filled on a spot near the Obiston shaft, and there were many volunteers to assist in filling it with hot air. "Every boy in Storey County was holding onto the ropes of the balloon, peering through rents at the bottom to look at the fire inside which furnished the hot air. The flames rose luridly from the brazier filled with pitch pine and petroleum. It required the combined profanity of the circus company to keep the boys away,"* reported the Chronicle's *man.*

*The balloonist, brilliant in blue tights with spangles, swung onto the trapeze, and the big bag begun to rise above the Comstock. After a brief flight, it descended near the Mint Mine, and five or six hundred of the throng who had watched the balloonist bought tickets and went into the main tent.*

*A week later, the balloonist who had escaped the vagaries of the Virginia City zephyrs was sailing over Carson City when the trapeze gave way.⁵*

A constant stream of commerce and communication filtered across the
Sierra Nevada between Virginia City and San Francisco—the Comstock's
spiritual home. Before the completion of the Virginia & Truckee
Railroad, stage lines provided the only link. Above, stages pick up men
and money from Wells Fargo express office; below, a California
Stage Company coach prepares to leave the International Hotel.

A view of C Street in 1877. The brand-new International Hotel
dominates the scene. The first International had been destroyed
in the fire of 1875; its successor was destined to burn in 1916.

# ALMOST
# AN ACTOR

EVERY MAN WHO EVER HAD ANY BOYHOOD once wanted to run away to sea or to go on the stage. After seeing my first melodrama, I came away from the theater wondering how I could be both sailor and actor. This was obviously impossible, but I hesitated to make a choice. In the end I became neither, and the world was spared the infliction of a poor sailor or a worse actor.

As I recall it now, my dream of the stage was the sweeter, fraught as it was with fond hopes and bitter disappointment. Once I came very near to taking a part in a real play. A cheap company had come to Virginia City with a repertoire long enough to last six nights and a matinee. The stage manager was the now famous William A. Brady. It hurts me to mention his name, even though years have passed since I yearned for the life of the stage.

To get on with the story, supes were needed for the production of *The Veteran*. These supes were to be clad in gorgeous red, blue, and yellow Zouave uniforms. It was the chance of my life. As I lined up with the other applicants against the scenery in the sacred part of Piper's Opera House, my heart was beating so hard it pained me.

Brady gave me one look, singled me out, and in the most matter-of-fact way pronounced these words of doom: "You won't do, kid. You're too small." I was certainly too small after he said that.

At the time of my awful humiliation, I vowed to get even with Brady. I did all in my power to injure him. The very next afternoon I slipped into one of his shows without paying. A side door had been left unguarded, and nine youngsters scampered in like a stampede of rabbits. Bob Morrison, the chief of police, sat still and smiled until we all got inside. Then he turned to a man closer to the opening and said, "I guess the kids are all in. You might as well close the door."

Bob was tax collector as well as chief of police, and when a few months later both he and ten thousand dollars of the tax money were missing, nine little sinners remembered his kindly dereliction of duty and openly expressed the hope that he would never be caught. He never was.

But that free show! It was a dramatization of Hugh Conway's novel *Called Back*, and at least nine of the audience found their keenest delight in trying to encore the supes. We knew them all. They were cast as serfs and had to drag wood by the sled-load to a Siberian convict camp. From the best seats that we could find, we noted each detail of the performance and made critical comments.

The supes brought in a load of wood, tossed it through a window in the scenery, and went out after another load. Pretty soon they dragged on the same number of sticks. "Nosey" Butler, who had taken possession of a seat a few rows in front of me, took one good look at the stage, then turned around and announced in a half whisper that could be heard all through the building, "Say, fellers, it's the same old load." No line in the play got the applause that followed Nosey's announcement.

One summer day Madame Janauschek came to town to present several plays, including *Macbeth*. A member of the gang told us that there was a "bully" duel in the piece; his dad had told him so. I wanted to see it, but I hadn't any money. "Nosey" Butler also wanted to see it. We saw it.

Talk about your cliff climbers! You should have seen us chasing up a ladder, creeping along a ridge of the opera house roof, disappearing through a skylight, and gingerly stepping from rafter to rafter in perhaps the gloomiest garret ever invaded by small boys.

The ceiling was not intended to be used as flooring, and we were running the risk of breaking through and falling about sixty feet into two-dollar seats. Nothing like that happened, however. We finally found seats on a great beam at least ten feet above the lofty perch occupied by the curtain-raisers.

If you never saw a play from above the stage, you can't appreciate its advantages. We watched the actors loafing between the flies, saw them dashing off the stage and then stopping as suddenly as if someone had yanked them with a lariat. But that wasn't all. Even the "bully" duel wasn't the best thing. We saw dead men get up and walk. This must have tickled Nosey, for he said, "That's more'n we'd get if we'd paid two dollars."

It wasn't always so easy for me. I could even put up with amateurs in those days, but when the local talent played *Under the Gaslight*, the skylight was battened down and I still had no money. We, the gang, stood around the entrance of the opera house talking out loud about it being a "rotten show" until the doorkeeper got exasperated and started after us with a section of gaspipe, which, unfortunately for us, happened to be handy. I was laughing so much I couldn't run, and he caught me. *Under the Gaslight* was an idyl of the Arcadian woods compared to what I got. I was under the gaspipe.

In a week I could walk around without feeling hurt, and I still wanted to be an actor. It was not to be. I never got any nearer to the stage than I was on the night I saw *Macbeth* from the rafters. My brother was more successful. He once buckled on armor and carried a spear in support of Frederick Warde.

# COMMENTARY

*William A. Brady[1] was no more than nineteen or twenty years old when he crushed Johnny's theatrical ambitions. He was touring with a company headed by J. R. Grismer, one of the oldtimers of the seventies and eighties. Brady acted as utility man as well as a member of the company and played as many as six roles in one* evening's performance. He was also the man to look after the props, line up supers, even watch the doorkeeper to be sure no one got in without a ticket. Brady had been working his way up in the theater and was quite willing to take Grismer's rigid training. Brady does not mention Virginia City in his autobiography but does recall having to hire four Piutes for supers when Winnemucca's white population turned him down during this tour with Grismer.

The play requiring supers in Zouave uniforms was written by John Lester Wallack,[3] a member of the famous English stage family. Wallack was an exceedingly popular and gifted actor in his time and wrote or adapted a number of plays besides The Veteran. He had long since taken over his father's theater and stage interests, and was a leader on the New York scene by the time Grismer's company came to Virginia City with six nights of repertoire, which included Called Back, The Two Orphans, Under the Gaslight, and possibly The Count of Monte Cristo. Called Back[4] was written by Conway in collaboration with J. Comyns Carr, author and manager for many years. Both were very young at the time. Conway died in 1885 at the age of thirty-seven, shortly after Called Back began a run at the Haymarket in London—a run that went through 219 performances. Carr himself died in 1916 at the age of sixty-seven.

By the time Johnny watched Called Back from gallery seats through the benign offices of Bob Morrison, the "new" opera house on B Street had been open nearly four years. Instead of the dark green upholstery of the old opera house—built by Tom Maguire down on D Street in 1867—Piper's had bright red plush, with gilded scroll work on the ceiling and boxes, and lace curtains to shield the antics of the occupants of those boxes from the curious.[5] Not more than a year from the time Brady appeared with Grismer's company, Piper's burned down for the second time.[6] The present building is the successor to the one in which Brady played Abbe Faria as well as Fernand in The Count of Monte Cristo.

Madame Francesca Romana Magdalena Janauschek,[7] whom Johnny saw as Lady Macbeth, was in her early fifties that summer day of 1882. She was the toast of Europe for her playing of tragic roles when she first came to the United States shortly after the end of the Civil War. It is said that when she first appeared opposite

*Edwin Booth in* Macbeth, *she spoke her lines in German while he responded in English. But by the time she appeared in Virginia City, she could speak English.*

Under the Gaslight,[8] *by famous playwright Augustin Daly, was that chilling perennial with the locomotive thundering down on the helpless hero as he lay tied to the track. Brady had to see to it that the sound and power of the engine worked at the same time that he was rushing on stage as Bermudas.*

*Frederick Warde*[9] *began touring with his own company in 1881, playing Shakespearean roles as well as* The Lady of Lyons, Virginius, *and* The Gladiators. *Johnny's younger brother George was probably a super in one of Warde's performances after the family moved to San Jose, California, in the late eighties. Warde did some Shakespeare for the early movies, became a lecturer and author on Shakespeare, and received an honorary degree from the University of Southern California for his scholarly achievements.*

"The people who built up Virginia City and gave it the greatness of the '70s," Waldorf said, "were the salt of the earth, and the breed has not died out." Some of the "breed" lined up on C Street in front of Beck's Store.

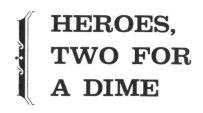

# HEROES, TWO FOR A DIME

I F TODAY SOMEONE WOULD OFFER ME a five-cent novel of adventure, I would turn up my nose and look insulted. In no other way could I express my contempt for that class of literature, but down in my heart I should feel guilty of rank ingratitude.

When I was a boy in Virginia City, the sixteen-page and thirty-two page pamphlet-like novels with a thrill or two on every page, and just the size to hide behind an open geography book, gave me countless hours of delight. It wasn't only in the reading that I found pleasure but in the hope of some day becoming a detective greater than "Old Neversleep," or an Indian fighter braver than "Moccasin Mose."

Lest anyone think that my ambition was narrow, I here record a confession that I wanted to be at least nine kinds of hero. I stood ready, or thought I did, to trail thieves, stop runaways, put down a mutiny on shipboard, rescue beautiful maidens from burning buildings, lead the palefaces against bloodthirsty redskins—in fact, do any and everything that might possibly make haughty folk say in admiring tones as I passed by, "There goes the boy hero." Of course, fate proved unkind. A boy may wander along in a happy-go-lucky way and happen to do something wonderfully brave, but just as sure as he camps on the trail of fame, he will find that he has been wasting his time.

The nearest I ever came to being a hero was when I responded to a dare by going through a dark wagon road tunnel at ten o'clock at night. To tell the truth I hated to do it, and even the defiant whistle that marked my progress failed to drive off the chill that settled upon me the moment I set foot into the darkness. However, the boy who did the daring couldn't see me shiver, and he gave me a reputation that I didn't deserve. Still it was all for the best. My reputation kept sending me into dark tunnels until I finally became so used to the experience that I forgot to get scared. About that time the boys came to the conclusion that I was a freak instead of a hero.

Meantime I found some joy by reading every five- or ten-cent shocker that I could borrow or buy. Often when the news dealer was a bit slow, I sent to New York for the latest. Once I got a dollar's worth at once, and as I lived the charmed lives of which I read, I was twenty kinds of hero in a single week. Then I lent my library, a book at a time, and brought on myself at least fifteen inglorious quarrels because only five of the twenty masterpieces ever came back.

Although I have long since reformed, I should like to read about Moccasin Mose again. He was the hero of my first five-cent novel. I bought him and *Ned Newton, the Young Engineer of the Swan* for a dime, and as I read of their exploits with a feverish interest that made me deaf to the cry of, "Johnny, supper's ready," a new world opened to me.

Moccasin Mose was surely a wonder. He dressed in a buckskin suit, wore a coonskin cap, and in order to live up to his name, boycotted the shoe dealer. I can't remember all he did, but he surely was the hope of the blockhouse that was besieged by countless red devils. It was a hot old fight. I find myself getting interested as I think of it.

"*Crack! Crack!*"

"*Whiz! Whiz!*"

Each side took two shots apiece for awhile, but as there was only a little band of palefaces and a mob of redskins, the arrows soon began to outnumber the bullets. No end of *whiz*zes were wasted, but every now and then an arrow got past a rifle and pinned a brave defender to the floor. This always made Moccasin Mose angry.

This trusty weapon said, "*Crack! Crack! Crack!*"—just like

that—and three redskins bit the dust. Finally the redskins got tired of biting the dust. All was quiet for a few minutes, and then blazing arrows began to fly through the air. The devils were trying to set fire to the blockhouse.

"*Crack! Crack!*" went the rifles, but the whizzers wouldn't quit. They just kept on with their deviltry, and it wasn't long before the hearts of the defenders began to sink. No wonder they were getting scared. They could hear the sound of flames crackling on the dry roof. All hope seemed lost. Everybody except Moccasin Mose was white with fear, and even he didn't see much chance of saving his scalp, but he was the real stuff of which heroes are made.

After a modest little speech, he climbed out on the roof in plain sight of the devils in the wood and began to pluck out the burning arrows one by one and throw them on the ground. The redskins yelled with rage. Mose couldn't hear anything but the whizzing. One arrow grazed his head; another passed through his sleeve. If he had not borne a charmed life, I would never have been able to read about him. He stayed on that roof until the fire was all out. As he went inside to give the defenders a chance to thank their preserver, it began to rain, and the redskins got disgusted and hurried off. That's all I remember of Moccasin Mose.

The other story, the one about Ned Newton, the Young Engineer of the *Swan*, lacked redskins but had something just as bad in a collection of gamblers called "blacklegs." Ned was a smart young fellow. While the other boys were going to school, he went to work on a Mississippi River steamboat and rose, not step by step, but in one big jump to the position of engineer.

While he was looking after things, no boat could beat the *Swan*, although the race was always awfully close, so close that I could feel the thrill clear to my toes. Ned never failed to get more speed at the critical time, even though he had to order part of the boat crammed into the furnace. Still his big hit wasn't made in the races. He laid out blacklegs like Moccasin Mose laid out redskins.

Once a blackleg who carried a sword cane tried to cheat one of Ned's friends out of everything he had in the world. "No you don't," said Ned, and then he and the blackleg fought. The sword cane almost pierced Ned's heart, but he dodged just in time, and what he did to the blackleg after that was something terrible. I forget where Ned landed in the last chapter, but it is my present impression that the owner of a fleet of riverboats took him into partnership and wouldn't let him put up a cent.

While recalling my boyhood heroes, I must not overlook "Old Neversleep." He was a greater detective than "Old Sleuth." Mystery was meat and drink and rest to him. When Scotland Yard and Inspector Byrnes said that the criminals would forever remain unknown, he would pitch in and prove that he was the kingpin of all the profession. After trying a dozen disguises, slipping into seven or eight robbers' dens, and tossing three or four rogues over his head, he ended up by trapping the whole bunch. Nobody could get ahead of Old Neversleep. Even the early bird hadn't a chance, for it isn't on record that the world's greatest detective ever went to bed. He was up all the time, and just before sunrise was one of his favorite hours for getting busy.

I repeat again that I have stopped reading shockers. It is many years since I educated myself beyond this form of dissipation, but my rebel conscience yet tells me that I am still in debt to the three wonderful heroes of my youth—Moccasin Mose, Ned Newton, and Old Neversleep.

# COMMENTARY

Ned Newton, the Young Engineer of the Swan, *and* Moccasin Mose[1] *seem to have disappeared into the mists of time—at least according to the Library of Congress, which could find no reference to them. But* Old Sleuth *and* Old Neversleep *have weathered the ravages of the years and now repose in prized library collections.*

Old Neversleep,[2] *by Walter Fenton, appeared in the first issue of the* Five Cent Weekly Library, *published by Frank Tousey of New York. It came out on December 25, 1883, when Johnny was thirteen. Old Sleuth*[3] *was the pseudonym of Harlan Page Halsey, who wrote a series which ran through 101 issues and was published quarterly between 1885 and 1905 by George Munro of New York. Many a lurid title of his appears in the Beadle Collection of Dime Novels*[4] *given to the New York Public Library by Dr. Frank P. O'Brien in 1922 and also among the dime novels included in Charles Bragin's* Dime Novels Bibliography, 1860–1928.

*The wagonroad tunnel*[5] *between Virginia City and Gold Hill was in constant use in the days before the Virginia and Truckee Railroad was completed in the fall of 1869. The* Territorial Enterprise *for February 4, 1870, notes: "Although the railroad runs side by side with it, the old Tunnel Toll Road is still a great deal navigated by quartz teams, principally by teams loaded with ore for mills at no great distance."*

The International Hotel in 1878, shortly after its completion.

Below is a view of the First International Hotel, before its destruction in the great fire of 1875. At the new hotel (see overleaf) John Mackay, one of the four Irish Comstock Kings—Mackay, William O'Brien, James Fair, and James Flood—took over the top floor for his Virginia City headquarters. His home had been destroyed by the same fire that burned down the original hotel. John Mackay (left) was a favorite of Johnny's for his open-handed contributions in front of Piper's Opera House. "We never envied John Mackay. We wanted him to live forever and always be rich." James G. Fair (right) was less popular—and apparently for good reason. One story had it that Fair responded to an injured miner's request for firewood by saying, "Send a load of blocks to that broken-backed pauper."

# THE
# RUNAWAY KID

A NY BOY CAN RUN AWAY, but it takes something besides desire to make the venture a success. Memory tells me that
I left Virginia City secretly about four times before I
graduated from the class known derisively as "little ten-day
bums." Twice I returned home of my own accord; once I went
back with Dad on one side of me and the constable on the other,
but the fourth time I kept on going.

My experiments in the runaway business covered a period of
eleven years, and I am vain enough to believe that I am quali-
fied to give expert testimony. Not that I am trying to prove
anything; far from it. There is nothing to prove unless it be that
no home can be made sufficiently attractive to change the mind
of the boy who lets his thoughts dwell on the big world beyond
the horizon. I wanted to run away so badly that I once tried to
get company for the walk across the hundred miles of desert
that lie between Virginia City and Austin. Luckily, the members of the gang to whom I appealed had more sense than I. If
they hadn't, I wouldn't be telling this story today. That trip
would have been too much for me, even if I had been the toughest
boy that ever smelt sagebrush.

After lack of encouragement had forced me to give up the
idea of walking to Austin, I turned my attention to getting
companions for a dash into the world by way of Reno, the
nearest station on the Overland railway. Success did not come
until after Dad and I had failed to agree on the important

question of whether he or I was the proper person to chastise brother George. During the argument he became excited and reached for me. I ran out of the house and standing on the hill about twenty feet from the door declined his urgent invitation to return and receive the reward which I richly deserved. I was in no hurry. Dad had to go to work in half an hour.

When he went away, shaking his head just as if somebody had angered him, I slipped into the house, grabbed an old hat, and hurried out again. I was ready to start for Reno, Madagascar, Patagonia, or the North Pole. It didn't matter much to me. I wanted to travel. As for funds, I considered myself amply supplied. I had a dollar and a quarter.

It took me nearly three days to get out of Virginia City. Companions for an aimless journey were hard to get. The first night I slept in the manger of a barn owned by a dear old man named McGrath. He didn't know he had a lodger, and I can still see his look of surprise when he looked down from the loft in the morning and saw me in time to save me from being buried under the cow's breakfast. He advised me to go home, but I merely changed my lodgings.

The second night I slept in an empty house in a pile of sawdust. This reminds me that sawdust makes an uncomfortable bed, and I now warn my friends against it. If you are ever forced to make a choice between sawdust and the cold ground, don't hesitate. Help yourself to as much ground as you need and stretch out. When I arose from my downless couch, I had sawdust in my ears, mouth, hair, and eyes. My pockets were full of it. Worse than that, it had worked inward as far as it could go, and I was the most uncomfortable kid in all Storey County. If Dad had come after me then I would have gone home, but he thought I would soon weary of depending on friends for food and was waiting hopefully for me to come back.

On the third day I found two boys who were willing to listen to my plan. I pictured the delights of a roving life and diplomatically mentioned that I had $1.25. One of the boys I shall call Mike and the other Bill. Mike had a dollar. When Mike displayed his wealth, Bill said, "You fellows are fixed. I can't go 'cause I ain't got a cent." This inspired me to resort to bribery. I volunteered to give Bill half a dollar if Mike would give him a quarter. "Do that," I argued, "and we'll have six bits apiece. That'll be plenty of money to get to California with."

Mike was duly impressed with the brilliancy of my scheme to finance the venture. Bill couldn't resist our magnificent offer, and for at least five minutes the three of us were equally rich. Bill at once got that opulent feeling. Although not more than seventeen years old, he had acquired an adult thirst for hard liquor, and as soon as his hand touched money his thirst began to assert itself.

Before we had reached the First Ward schoolhouse, which wasn't more than half a mile from the scene of our compact, Bill blurted out, "Let's get a quarter's worth of booze." That "let's" was merely politeness. Mike and I protested, but Bill bought the booze. He allowed us each a swallow, and then, because we choked a little, he called us kids and asked us to observe how a thoroughbred drank whiskey. We were then out on the road to Reno, but Virginia City wasn't more than half a mile behind us when Bill finished the flask.

We walked along until we reached a roadhouse five miles from town. The very sight of the place must have set Bill's thirst to jumping again, for he immediately turned to us and said decisively: "Let's get another quarter's worth of booze." This investment left Bill with a total capital not much larger than he possessed when we took him into partnership. He managed to get enough strength from the second flask to carry him the seven miles downgrade to Floyd's. There we heard the same old suggestion, "Let's get another quarter's worth of booze." The third flask reduced Bill from opulence to beggary.

While we were resting at Floyd's, he finished his final installment of booze and began to complain of hunger. I wasted a quarter on bread and cheese. After eating heartily, Bill remarked: "We ought to have something to wash this down with." Mike and I pointed the way to the water barrel, and Bill scowled and called us kids again.

By this time night had come, and we asked the landlord's boy if we could sleep in the big barn that was almost filled with loose hay. After consulting with father, young Floyd informed us that our wish would be gratified provided we would promise not to smoke in the barn. We solemnly promised. We crawled into the hay, and about three minutes after I heard Bill's husky voice asking for a match. "Here," answered Mike, "Have you got the makin's?"

Before they went to sleep, Bill and Mike smoked four cigarettes apiece. This necessitated the lighting of half a dozen matches, but luck was with us and we escaped disaster. I took no part in the offending, but I can hardly claim credit for superior virtue. I never did like cigarettes.

In the morning we walked to the first ranch, and there Mike begged breakfast for the party. After that nothing would do but a dip in one of the unfenced warm water springs at Steamboat. To do this we wasted four hours and walked two unnecessary miles. By this time we were hungry again, and Bill beat me drawing straws to determine which one of us would beg dinner for all three.

It was my first attempt. I went to the kitchen door and told the lady who answered my knock that we had not eaten for forty-eight hours. The lady from the first ranch happened to be visiting the second ranch. She had seen the three of us, and when she came into the kitchen with hands upraised in horror at the magnitude of my falsehood, I almost ran through the fence. I succeeded in beating the dog to the gate. That experience cured me of begging. I wasn't a success at it.

We kept on going until we reached Reno, nine miles from the ranch where we didn't eat. An investment of seventy-five cents brought each of us a square meal, after which Mike and I quarreled with Bill because he insisted on "another quarter's worth of booze."

A boxcar on a sidetrack was our lodging house that evening. The next day we spent half a dollar for food, and our syndicate was penniless. Bill declared for a swift journey homeward. Mike was half willing to turn back, but I was bent on going on. I scurried around and found a shipper who promised me free transportation to California if I would assist in chaperoning a trainload of sheep. I accepted the offer, and then out of pure malice Bill tried to rob me of my opportunity. As I stood beside the shipper on the rear platform of the caboose, Bill cried out, "Don't take him, mister. He's runnin' away." I could feel my heart leaving me. A second of agony, and then—the shipper smiled, the train moved, and I wiggled my fingers at Bill.

It was years before I saw Dad again, but I didn't make my fortune. Still, I was proud of myself. No one could ever again point the finger of scorn and call me a "little ten-day bum."

# COMMENTARY

*Although it turned out that Johnny Waldorf liked to dream about the ocean far more than he enjoyed this one venture on it as a "cabin boy," he used to sit on the back steps of the house on G Street and try to imagine that the view beyond Sugar Loaf resembled the sea he had never seen. Somehow when he gazed on the rolling clouds, he thought of breaking waves, and the lavender mists of the Forty-Mile Desert were like the ocean. But even he had to agree that the Forty-Mile Desert would have killed him. It had made life a misery for many an overland emigrant, and as late as the 1880s one could find scattered relics of those tortured covered wagon trains which so long ago had dragged themselves across the alkali wastes parched for water.*

*He always told of his last experience in running away with great tenderness. "Dear old Mr. McGrath" had peered down into the hay as he asked in mild-voiced surprise, "Why Johnny, what yuh doin' there?" There was always a quizzical expression on his face as he told his children about Mr. McGrath, and honey in his voice. If Johnny had not been so determined to end all possibility of being called a "little ten-day bum," it is probable that he would have taken Mr. McGrath's advice and gone home to face his father. McGrath's was only a few blocks from his home.*

*The First Ward School was built in early 1875. It stood out on*

North C Street and was used by relief committees for the care of refugees of the Great Fire, which did not get that far north of town. The building referred to by Waldorf as a roadhouse five miles from town was the Five-Mile House, a bar and rest spot that stood a mile from the point near where the present Gieger Grade turns away (possibly with a shudder) from the remnants of the old grade plunging down into Newton Canyon.

The Geiger Toll Station at the foot of the perilous old grade was the largest tollhouse on the way from Reno to Virginia City. It was surrounded by a settlement of some size at the end of a handsome dell into which the exhausted travelers and the weary truckers drove after the final twist and dive of the steep old grade was passed. West of it stretched a row of poplar trees, survivors of which were still standing in 1956, according to Walter Mulcahy, authority on the old roads of western Nevada. Floyd's was probably the farm, big barn, corrals, wagon yard, and blacksmith shop which stood a little way from the tollhouse. There was also an inn and restaurant for the overnight traveler, which at one time was known as the Magnolia House.

The ranch where Mike begged breakfast for the trio could have been that of George Ritter. At the Windmill Saloon on the way to Steamboat Valley, one had to turn south about a half mile to reach the Ritter ranch, which covered eighty acres, partly wild, partly in spring wheat, and partly in truck gardens, including marvelous potatoes that John Waldorf remembered with nostalgia in after years.

The original Geiger Toll Road apparently turned north at Boilling Springs, breaking into three parts. One part went south to the Steamboat Springs Resort, which lay about three miles west and south of the tollhouse. At one time or another, the other two roads led to Stone and Gates Crossing and to Lakes Crossing, which by Johnny's time was the thriving town of Reno.

Somewhere along the way to Boiling Springs, the boys turned off to hunt for a warm-water pool. Wherever they found it, they most certainly must have heard the Boiling Springs thumping and pumping like a steamboat coming around the bend. Steam rose chuckling and whistling from the encrusted and riven ground. Off to the west of the warm spring where the boys swam was the Steam-

*boat Springs Resort, probably still owned by John and Matt Rapp.*

*The ranch at which Johnny made his one try at begging a meal may have been that of James Gregory, an oldtimer, or it could have been that of Granville W. Huffaker, who had come to the head of Truckee Meadows to farm back in 1858. His ranch was seven miles south of Reno, a figure close to the nine miles that John Waldorf recalled, purely by guesswork.*

Bowers Mansion (above), now a historical museum, was the site of picnicking for Johnny and his friends. The James G. Fair home (below) inspired endless speculation regarding the whereabouts of great piles of gold coins.

# BACK
# TO THE
# OLD HOME

W HEN, AFTER A LONG ABSENCE, a man goes back to the town of his boyhood, he is expected to return to the world mourning his last and sweetest illusions. I had supposed the rule to be infallible, but I know better now. Expecting little and prepared for bitter disappointment, I took a vacation trip to Virginia City, the one place which my memory had hallowed. A few days ago, I left the old familiar scenes, and as I looked back from the car window and saw the sunbeams gilding Mount Davidson, I was still a boy, and the throb of my heart told me that my illusions were a part of my life.

I shall never forget that vacation journey to the mining camp that had held me captive for thirteen golden years of youth. Often in those bygone days I had fretted like a prisoner, but the great world had taught me that only childhood knows true liberty, and I went back to Virginia City with the chastened spirit of the prodigal.

Time dragged until the train reached Reno. Then I began to grow young again. Reno always figured in my itinerary in the days when I was a "runaway kid." No sooner had I left the train than I thought of the time when I walked Reno's streets ringing a bell and informing the populace of an impending auction. My employer had given me instructions rather hastily, and after I got started I was not positive whether the auction was to be held next door to the "Wine House" or the "White House." Rather than go back, I compromised. First I shouted

"Wine House," and then I shouted "White House," keeping it up impartially for half an hour. Then one of the oldest inhabitants called me aside and told me that the liquor establishment was the neighbor of the auction house. I thanked him, did the right thing for fifteen minutes then quit the job.

Getting back to the present, I saw passenger cars inscribed "Virginia and Truckee Railroad" and at once drifted off again into the past. As I sped through Truckee Meadows, I imagined myself plodding along the dusty road toward Reno, hungry but hopeful, and wondering if the boys would ever let up on me if I had to go home to eat.

Soon the train was among the hills, the dear old hills with the dull brocade of sagebrush. Hills gave way to mountains. We followed the winding course of the Carson River for miles. Then came the great, wide sweep of hills that never fails to delight the eye. The air is clear, and one can see for miles. Hills seem to be piled on hills, mountains upon mountains. The train makes the letter S and the letter U over and over again. Horseshoe bends are too common for distinction. We climb steadily as we creep around the slopes, and soon tunnels on the hillside and heaps of waste rock tell us that we have reached the mining country.

I had been away for a score of years, but everything had a familiar look. Silver City nestled far down the canyon; Gold Hill still held precarious foothold beside the steep road; the Crown Point bridge had lost none of its forbidding height; and but for the absence of some of the landmarks of other days, I might have imagined that I had been gone only a night. Gold Hill brought up only one regret—that I had once wasted precious hours there while I was supposed to be in school in Virginia.

The train passed through three tunnels, all a little shorter than my memory had pictured, and I was back again in the place of my early joys. I had thought to find it a wreck, but there it stood, smaller, it is true, yet still holding a thousand things to recall the adventures of childhood. The orehouse from which I fell in my haste to be the first one down; the hills over which I clambered; the slum pond on which I ran races and was invariably beaten; the dumps on which I had worn out my shoes; the great mountain that stood guard over the camp; that odd-looking hill, Sugar Loaf, keeping aloof from its fellows—all these were there to gladden my eyes. It did not matter that a mammoth pile of gray waste rock hid the backyard that had contained my circus. I was too happy at what I found to mourn what I missed.

For the greater part of five days I wandered over the town renewing my youth. As I looked upon Alexander's lot, fancy covered it again with big white tents, and I could almost hear the roaring of the "lines and taggers." The old swimming pond was gone, but there was a new one not far off.

As for the mines, several hoisting works had disappeared, many were idle, but the most surprising change of all was the silence of those that were still in operation. Up-to-date mining seems to minimize noise. I used to go to sleep to the clang of machinery and the puffing of steam, and only the cessation of the clamor could wake me up before Mother called me in the morning. Now all is different. The mines do their work quietly, and one can stand outside the great frame building and hear no more noise than is made by the printing presses of a big news-paper. Perhaps it is the silence that makes many of the old-timers think that the town is dead.

The truth is that the camp is better off now than it was twenty years ago. Then it was on the downgrade. Now, with up-to-date mining and new ore bodies in sight, the future is bright with hope. Even at present there are five hundred men at work, which is more than any other camp in the state can boast. In the words of an expert mining man, Virginia does not depend upon the prospecting of cabbage patches but has a true fissure vein that promises treasure as vast as that which has already been taken from the depths beneath its streets. As for myself, I venture to predict that within the next eighteen months new dwelling houses will be built on the Comstock, something which has not happened since I was barefoot.

And now to resume the story of my visit. Virginia may change, but its people remain the same, always kind, always spending their money with easy grace, always keeping their doors open to both friend and stranger. They made me feel as though I had never left home but had simply slept away the years and awakened among the folks who had known me as a boy. We were all children of a larger growth.

Companions of my school days had followed in the footsteps of their fathers and, like them, had become brave miners who face death with a laugh. Others had gone into business. One of these was George Hester, whom I discovered dealing in groceries, the brand of whiskey recommended by Abe Ruef, and as fine a line of blarney as can be found anywhere. I mention this merely because Hester may some day become a famous promoter of trusts, and I want to be able to say to my friends, "I told you so."

One thing that I missed in Virginia was the Indian camps. There are a few left, but most of the Piutes have died or departed, and nearly all of those who remain prefer a battered shanty to a wigwam. Some of the squaws have sewing machines in their homes. Civilization has done its worst. The Piute Indian is no longer interesting.

Before my vacation ended, I went on a moonlight picnic to Bowers' Mansion, where many, many years ago I fell into a mud puddle and carried off about nine pounds of Washoe County's most valuable soil. This time I managed to keep my feet, but I noticed a few staggering strangers who needed only a puddle to duplicate my experience. While at the picnic grounds, I donned a bathing suit and went in swimming. No sooner had I hit the water than a kid on the bank shouted, "How is it, Fatty?" and as I sputtered "Fine," I felt as though my tenth birthday had come back to me.

# COMMENTARY

*There was a tumult of planning and packing for that visit back to the old town. Midget was going along, but she had never before left the three children for such a long time—an entire week. "Mother Waldorf" was appealed to and came up from San Jose, not without some foreboding. One of the relatives had remarked in her hearing that John's children were "just like three little Indians." But all arrangements were made, the children counseled to be on their best behavior, and the travelers were off. They arrived in Virginia City on September 16, 1905. Midget was prepared to be amazed, and she was.*

*The original Wine House in Reno was owned by E. Chielovich and burned in the great Reno fire of March 3, 1879. It was probably the second Wine House, which Chielovich built next door to the White House Auctioneers somewhere along Commercial Row, that caused all Johnny's confusion. The big Reno fire was almost as bad as that which had swept Virginia City in 1875. It had destroyed 350 buildings at a property loss of a million dollars, leaving the town "a suburb without a city,"[1] according to one report.*

*The Virginia and Truckee Railroad car which John Waldorf boarded with Midget at Reno in 1905 had originally been painted green but had been changed to canary yellow sometime during the years. The rest of the train was probably just as it had been in his boyhood; on sunny days the arched, church-like windows with their stained glass tops cast colored lights on the passengers, and the oil cloth ceilings, the chenille upholstery, and the woodwork were all probably just a little darkened by time. The glass windows, however, were clear enough for Midget to see the maddening curves and twists, the deep canyons on the ride to Virginia City. No matter what time may have done to the interior of the cars, the red and gold locomotives were as brilliant and tenderly polished as ever. The train probably had its usual complement of cars, a couple of baggage cars, an express car, and several passenger cars. In Septem-*

ber 1905, the line had thirty-two years and ten months left of existence, but its decline had begun in 1880 when Johnny was ten and
the Silver City tracks had been pulled up for the Carson and
Colorado Narrow Gauge. The Virginia Evening Chronicle had
sadly commented that "This is rough on Silver [City] and looks
like the abandonment of that sagebrush metropolis to the coyote and
the Piute." The headline mourned: "Switching Off A City."[2]

The Crown Point Trestle was 350 feet long and 90 feet high,
built across a steep ravine. It must have looked no less formidable
to the man than it had to the boy of the seventies and eighties on
those rides to Treadway's and Bowers' Mansion. Long since vanished, the Crown Point Trestle is immortalized on the seal of the
State of Nevada.

The final train on the Virginia and Truckee to Virginia City
was a special for the Chicago and Pacific Coast chapters of the
Railroad and Locomotive Historical Society in July 1938. The
slowly shrinking tunnels between Gold Hill and Virginia City
were so low that the passenger cars had to be left at Gold Hill, and
the travelers crept into the famous mining camp on flat cars. (Originally, the tunnels had been twelve feet high and fifteen feet wide.)

Bowers' Mansion was the palatial and imposing dream castle
built in Washoe Valley by Sandy (Lemuel) and Eilly Orum
Bowers with some of their early Comstock wealth. The money ran
through their fingers all too soon. They furnished the house lavishly
and traveled in Europe, but when Sandy died in 1868, he left poor
Eilly with more debts than she could ever pay. Although she was
said to have had some title to the house when she died in 1903, she
had not lived in it for years, and all the furnishings had long since
been sold to meet debts.

Nat Holmes seems to have been operating the mansion as a
family picnic resort in the late seventies and eighties, but it passed
through many hands over the years. Mr. and Mrs. Henry Ritter
bought the house shortly after Eilly's death and may have been
negotiating for the sale at the very time that John Waldorf walked
the half mile through moist meadows from the train stop to the old
house in the fall of 1905. The Ritters did not sell the mansion until
1946 when a drive initiated by Reno clubwomen and Washoe
County raised the $100,000 necessary to make the purchase.

*Today, the mansion is an historic building and museum, property of Washoe County. Many of the former furnishings and art objects have been restored. Children swim in the pools, and picnics are spread under the Lombardy poplars just as they were in Johnny's boyhood and as they were when he returned. But the poplars, likened in the seventies by a grumpy* Chronicle *reporter to "bean poles," have grown to gigantic size.*

*It was inevitable that John Waldorf should find some comrades of his boyhood lying among the silent company on Cemetery Hill. Sometime during the five days in Virginia City, his elder sister, Minnie Alice, guided them to the grave of their little sister Gertrude and to those of vanished playmates. Later, they visited the mother of one of those dead playmates. She was little and wiry, and she welcomed the big man with exuberant tenderness and tears.*

*"All my boys died," she told Midget with a quaver in her voice as she reached up to rub a thin caressing arm across John Waldorf's broad shoulders. "Nothin' could kill the damn girls!"*

*As painful as the visit was in some respects, Waldorf would return twice more before his death, and on his last visit would pen a moving tribute to the vanished town of his youth.*

In the view of Eliot Lord, Virginia City was "set in a desert with something prisonlike in its encircling wall of barren hills." The city is seen here looking north across the Combination shaft. For Waldorf, the town was a wonderland on the sunrise side of Mount Davidson.

Johnny Waldorf's house is among those at the right, on the street beyond the t
steeple of St. Mary's-in-the-Mountains. The pond where the boys often swam is i
area below the mine works in the background, extreme left.

# L'ENVOI

A FEW WEEKS AGO I went to Virginia City for my third visit in the thirty-eight years that have passed since the school-day morning I walked determinedly past the old First Ward School and slipped out over the Geiger Grade, running away to California. I had not seen the old town in nineteen years, and much of it had disappeared, but somehow memory took a dearer hold on what was left.

I had to tread the broken sidewalks gingerly, but it was my town, and I was proud of it. The Corporation House, perched on the mountainside, still held watch and ward. The Fourth Ward School was spick and span, its age hidden under a good coat of paint, and looking as if it had borrowed youth from each of the generations of school children it had sheltered.

At the north end of the long street that we knew so well, I found the First Ward School, weatherbeaten and weary and none too certain of its footing. The mere sight of it brought back to me the brief year I spent within its walls, a year that was a long battle to determine whether I or the principal should set the standards of order and discipline. In the course of the campaign one teacher lost his job and I, by special request, lost several weeks of schooling. I was confident then that all the right was on my side, but I'm not so sure now.

As I wandered back toward the Divide, something not at all suggestive of schools caught my eye. On C Street, almost in the shadow of the Corporation House, I saw an abandoned store with its iron shutters tightly closed. Above the door I read

J. B. DAZET, WINES AND LIQUORS, and my mind ran back to Madam Pantaloon, who used to sit there dozing but would wake suddenly when you came in and draw you something from your favorite wine barrel. Madam used to say that a little good wine wouldn't hurt anyone. As a boy I took her word for it, and I still think she was right.

My quest for old landmarks went on, and soon I found several houses, outside of which I used to stand and whistle, or shout—I wasn't much of a whistler—for some boyhood companion to come out. These houses all bore the marks of age, some leaned heavily on the downhill end, but most of them still served as homes. It was different with three houses that I at one time and another had called home. All were gone, and of two of them I couldn't find so much as an excavation. The mining dumps, like advancing waves, had long ago swept over them.

Somewhere under thousands of tons of waste lay the cellar that I helped to dig when Mrs. Bowers, the "Washoe Seeress," told my dear mother there was treasure under the house. I can still recall my blistered hands, but I have no regrets because for days I spent imaginary millions and was richer then than I have ever been since.

So it was that as I stood on C Street and looked down the hill, memories crowded fast upon me. The bright Nevada sun burnished the relics, and to me nothing was squalid. There was the fragment of the great brick stack that once marked the Savage hoisting works. There were the dumps on which I had once raced to tag wood so wet that it had to be dried in the oven before it could be used as fuel. Further down, Sugar Loaf yet loomed as in the days long gone. On the hills I could see the roads that once ran to Number 4 and Number 3, abandoned shafts that were to have given air to the Sutro Tunnel. These and a hundred other things I saw. It was the old town after all, and decades of misfortune had not robbed it of its charm.

Then there was the greater attraction, a little band of old schoolmates who gave me the prodigal's welcome, taking me back into the fold with an easy kin-like kindness that made my heart warm to them anew. And, after all, why not? They, too, could recall the days of Alexander's lot, and the gleam and glitter, and the elephants, and the canvas walls we used to slip under. They had seen the parades of the guards, the Emmets, the Nationals, the Washingtons, the Montgomerys, the Saarsfields, the "Tigers," the cannons of Battery B, and "Kittle Belly" Brown's red-shirted firemen. I had but to say a word to them to call up visions of Captain Peter Dunne proudly leading the Emmets on the Fouth of July and the long, rangy seven-foot Captain Salix striding along at the head of the "Tigers."

Their minds, like mine, went back to the Centennial Day when Nevada's first native-born white girl and boy took seats of honor on the pilot of a locomotive in Gold Hill and rode into Virginia City to start the festivities of the day. Like me, these old friends could go still further back and see the flames leaping from house to house and from street to street, climbing the steeples and burning on and on until two-thirds of Virginia lay in ashes.

I and my dear friends heard the old voices and saw the old faces again, but there was more than common memories to our momentarily renewed friendship. The concord of it all, the fact that we still had a feeling of kinship after all those years, were dividends to us from the people who built up Virginia City and gave it the greatness of the seventies. They were the salt of the earth, and the breed has not died out.

And the old town is far from gone yet. A world, pulling itself together after a demoralizing war [World War I], grows hungrier for the gold and silver on which stability depends. Perhaps in the train of that growing demand will come new shafts, more gloryholes and great mills, and the long-looked for boom come at last, not only come but stay and another wonder city rise on the steeps of old Mount Davidson. It may even be possible that alligators will play again in a hot water pond at the mouth of Sutro Tunnel!

And yet, come what may, we shall always hold close and deep our memories of Virginia, the town of our early joys, the town of friends who never forget, the town that we shall recall with smiles and sighs and tears so long as a stick or stone remains and the sagebrush grows at the foot of the dumps.

# COMMENTARY

*Virginia City was deep in decline by the time John Taylor Waldorf wrote his final tribute in 1924. It was by no means his last visit to the old town. There are scattered notes mentioning friends whom he found on occasional later trips to Virginia City, still picking away in shaft and tunnel, still looking for that lost bonanza. But after "L'Envoi" was written and slipped among his papers, his formal farewell was over. It was found eight years later, after his death.*

*During the years after he and his sister Minnie Alice had first retraced the paths of childhood across the town in 1905, her younger daughter, Reta, had been crowned queen of the golden jubilee of the Comstock in 1909. She had reviewed the grand parade in ermine and velvet coronation robes while the glory of the bonanza spirit glowed in every heart. Surely another boom would soon be resounding with the pounding and the roaring and the whistling of hoisting works and mills on the slopes of Mount Davidson! The* Virginia Evening Chronicle *was predicting a large work ahead, quite soon: "The Comstock is on the eve of better days." This promise was "the conviction of unbiased mining men who have given it attention."[1]*

*By 1924, Minnie Alice was a widow, living down at the Bay. Her four children were married and scattered to other parts of the country. So John Waldorf walked alone, gingerly, carefully, among the ruins of a town and its dying dreams.*

*The Fourth Ward School, which Johnny never seems to have attended, was dedicated on November 28, 1876. It still stands near the south end of C Street, not far from the Divide. Shored up and empty, it seems to be waiting for restoration as a museum and memorial to Young America.*

*The First Ward School disappeared between 1924 and the present, a victim of time and the zephyrs. It may have been the last school Johnny attended, and his battle with the principal may have been merely a means of impressing the very tough Andes or First Ward gangs with how really tough a Savage Gang member could be.*

*(Moving from one gang to another could never have been a peaceful occasion.) Most of the school years of the Waldorf children seem to have been spent at the Third Ward School down near the Catholic church.*

*Mrs. Lemuel (Sandy) Bowers, the Washoe seeress who predicted treasure for the Waldorfs, was a frequent visitor to Virginia City in the late seventies and eighties. Carrying her peep stone or crystal ball, she appeared from time to time in the town, escaping from her bleak basement flat near O'Farrell and Larkin streets in San Francisco to stay with a twice-widowed friend of Gold Canyon days, Mrs. George Dettenreider, who kept a rooming house on C Street.*

*Mrs. Bowers' second sight wrought miracles, if the stories in the* Enterprise *are a sampling of her achievements. She saw missing men dead at the bottom of old shafts. She even talked with the departed spirit of a man named Joe, buried in an unmarked grave on Cemetery Hill. Joe wished her to ask people of Virginia City to consult Messrs. Wilson and Brown, undertakers, to learn the exact position of his grave so that flowers could be put there on Decoration Day. Mrs. Bowers declared that he had told her, "If you could see the thousands of disembodied spirits hovering over the cemetery on that occasion, you would feel amply repaid for your trouble." The odd part of this matter, the* Enterprise *concluded, was that Mrs. Bowers hadn't even known Joe was dead.*[2]

*Sam Wagner, the town crier, once went through the streets ringing his bell and crying the offer of a $100 reward to anyone who could find a diamond ring lost by its owner on her way from the Wells Fargo office. The ring was worth no less than $450, according to the* Enterprise, *but it was not found until Mrs. Bowers was consulted. She calmly reassured the frantic woman, telling her that the ring would be returned without the thief being seen. Sure enough, the door bell rang one day, and when the good lady went to the door, there was an envelope with her ring in it.*[3]

*And there was Mr. G. L. Whitney, who had lost a valuable and ornate watch chain some four months past and had accused a former servant, a Chinese. When Mrs. Bowers returned to Virginia City, he called on her as a last resort. She advised him to search in some rubbish in one of the rooms of his home, and there it was.*

*What is more, Mr. Whitney announced to an* Enterprise *reporter that he would be "willing to sign an affidavit as related above."*[4]

*More than once the hopes of the Comstock were sustained by the Washoe seeress. In June of 1878 her second sight told her that one of the big Havana lottery prizes would come to Nevada the next time. And in December of the same year, Mrs. Bowers saw "blazing stars, a full moon, and lesser lights over the North End [of the Comstock]."*[5] *It seems that Mrs. Bowers had been having visions of a woman coming toward her in the night, leading little children. Banners were flying about her on which were the words "Sierra Nevada" and "Ophir," but, strangely enough, on the woman's back there was seen a "skeleton-like interweaving of veins." This, Mrs. Bowers assumed, was undiscovered silver, but a definite note of destruction was introduced when the woman was suddenly knocked down—which surely symbolizes what happened to the Sierra Nevada stock. Nevertheless, the* Enterprise *insisted that Mrs. Bowers had great faith in the North End. She was confident that "more large ore bodies will be discovered there soon."*

*It was probably long after the collapse of the Ophir boom in 1877, and not many months after the failure of Jacob D. Waldorf's railroad bill at Carson City, that Mrs. Bowers told Addie about the treasure under their house. This was no doubt after they had moved to a place somewhere near the Con-Virginia Hoisting Works, for by 1882 the great Savage Dump was fast encroaching on the little cottage at 175 South G Street.*

*James "Kettle Belly" Brown, who delighted the boys, was twice chief of the Virginia City fire department. He was the second chief of volunteers in 1873 and the first chief of the paid department in 1876. He listed himself in Bishop's Directory, 1878–79, as Chief James Brown, and this is confirmed by Wells Drury in* An Editor on the Comstock Lode, *but the chief's nickname, given for an obvious reason, made many forget the James. He was even referred to formally as "K. B." Brown. The spelling "Kittle Belly" is John Waldorf's phonetic recollection of a small boy's pronunciation.*

*Kettle Belly Brown was the very spirit of the Comstock. A former faro dealer in a saloon on the Divide, a plunger, a fancier of gamecocks, and a man of vivid imagination and colorful speech, he won*

*the affection of all, even though he was the target of many a sly
remark in the papers. Kettle Belly believed in the art of drinking
and eating with leisure and elegance, and had the greatest contempt
for those who did not practice the art.*

*He was a man of immediate impulse and picturesque outlook.
He lived the part of a paternal tyrant every moment of his years as
a chief, "growling like an earthquake"⁶ when the assistant engineer,
Joe Bell, and the twelve good men and true rehearsed for a demonstration of prowess in shooting a jet of water over Miners' Union
Hall or the flagpole of the International Hotel—suddenly lowering
his voice when ladies came within hearing. And when the men were
exhibiting their skill for the board of aldermen or the fire commissioners, Chief Brown could be seen walking up and down the street
"with as proud a smile as if he had purchased 40,000 shares of
Bodie at six bits a share."*

*Kettle Belly's assistant, Joe Bell, was about as heavy a man as
his chief, and once when an* Enterprise *reporter wanted to give an
idea of the width of a new door at the City Hall, recently converted
from an engine house, he wrote that the door was "sufficiently wide
to allow the entrance of the most corpulent member of our Board
of Aldermen. Chief Brown of the Fire Department and his first
assistant Joe Bell are able to pass through the door comfortably by
going one abreast."⁷*

*Kettle Belly was a favorite of newspaper writer Wells Drury,
who may have been the reporter who interviewed him for the San
Francisco* Examiner *in 1893 following a rumor that the mines were
to be pumped out and reworked. "I'll stand on C Street in front of
the Sawdust Corner and welcome back the prodigals," Kettle Belly
told the reporter. "Where would the Palace Hotel be, I'd like to ask,
if it hadn't of been for the bullion of the Comstock Lode? Where
would the Nevada Bank get off, and what would become of the
Flood Building? Wasn't the Mills Building put up with profits
from the Virginia and Truckee Railroad, and didn't the Comstock
furnish all the ore and most all the freight to give those profits?
What made Sutro Heights? The Comstock. What built those lordly
palaces of architectural splendor on Nob Hill? The Comstock. Who
put the postal cable lines across the continent and under the ocean?
The Comstock. What gave Uncle Sam his piles of gold to buy am-*

*munition and hard tack when the ark of the nation was buffeted by
the war billows of the greatest rebellion ever known in history? The
Comstock. What kept the Bank of California from going up the
flume? The Comstock!"*

*Kettle Belly concluded his defiant statement with a refusal to call
off the roll of all the Comstockers in town. "It would take too long.
I am just alluding to references I could make if I had a mind to say
something about the glories of the old Comstock Lode that John
Mackay is about to rejuvenate. They'll come from Europe, Asia
and Africa, Australia and the ends of the world!*[8]

*Virginia Tilton, one of the two first white children born in Ne-
vada, was the daughter of J. H. Tilton, who came to Virginia City
in 1859. She was born on April 1, 1860, in the house her father had
built on what would later be the site of Tom Maguire's Opera House
at D and Union streets. The girl was named after the mining camp
and was sixteen when on July 4, 1876, Centennial Day, she shared
the parade honors with Mark Bryan, Jr., another 1860 baby and
the son of a member of the territorial legislature. Virginia wore a
riding habit of patriotic colors with a lace and flowered headdress.
The youngsters rode at the head of the procession.*

*It was a brave parade with floats called "cars of state" drawn by
brewery horses trembling over the streets between rows of pine and
cedar "liberty trees" decked with flying flags, streamers of red,
white, and blue, and hung with lanterns. A large flag snapped and
furled at the top of Cedar Hill, and when night came, all the lanterns
along the streets glowed mellowly in the shadows. Up on top of
Mount Davidson a great bonfire of six cords of wood blazed while
fireworks, donated by James G. Fair, burst into brilliant explosions
until the whole mountain seemed afire.*

*Lazily steaming water still issues from under the closed gates of
the Sutro Tunnel far below Virginia City in the ghost town
of Sutro. Not only alligators, but trout and suckers and fish of
other species were planted at one time or another in the warm waters
at the mouth of the pool. But today the water grasses seem to be the
only living things in the quiet stream as it winds away toward no-
where in a world of blasted dreams, where even the trees stand bare,
and dying buildings lean wearily against nothing as they slowly
yield to the years.*

# NOTES

## Introduction   (pp. 1–35)

1. De Quille, Dan, *The Big Bonanza*, New York, 1947, p. 159.
2. *Ibid.*, p. 259.
3. Lord, Eliot, *Comstock Mining and Mines*, p. 381.
4. *Ibid.*, p. 441.
5. *Virginia Evening Chronicle*, November 9, 1880, p. 3.
6. Angel, Myron, *History of Nevada*, p. 327.
7. *Virginia Evening Chronicle*, March 6, 1879, p. 3; March 7, p. 3.
8. *Ibid.*, March 7, 1879, p. 3.
9. Angel, Myron, *op. cit.*, pp. 317, 326–27.
10. *Territorial Enterprise*, October 1, 1880, p. 2; November 9, 1880, p. 1; *Virginia Evening Chronicle*, September 30, 1880, p. 3.
11. Angel, Myron, *op. cit.*, p. 312.
12. *Virginia Evening Chronicle*, January 25, 1881, p. 3.
13. *Virginia Evening Chronicle, loc. cit.*
14. *Ibid.*, February 1, 1881, p. 3.
15. *Ibid.*, February 17, 1881, p. 3.
16. *Ibid.*, February 24, 1881, p. 3.
17. San Jose *Mercury*, May 27, 1896, p. 1.
18. San Francisco *Chronicle*, August 16, 1898, p. 1; Thomas S. Duke, *Celebrated Criminal Cases of America*, p. 133.
19. Older, Fremont, *My Own Story*, p. 52.
20. Wells, Evelyn, *Fremont Older*, p. 174.
21. Duffus, Robert L., *Tower of Jewels*, p. 181.
22. *Ibid.*, p. 70.

## The Strenuous Small Boy   (pp. 50–55)

1. *Territorial Enterprise*, July 12, 1878, p. 1.
2. *Ibid.*, June 23, 1878, p. 1.
3. San Francisco *Chronicle*, October 27, 1875, p. 3; for Dan de Quille's authorship, see Oscar Lewis introduction to *The Big Bonanza*.

## Kings of the Comstock   (pp. 60–65)

1. Lord, Eliot, *op. cit.*, p. 382.
2. *Constitution, By Laws, Order of Business and Rules of Order of the Miners' Union of Virginia, Nevada* (Virginia City, Nevada, 1879).

## Great Men I Have Known   (pp. 68–73)

1. V & T *Directory*, 1873–74, p. 15; Angel, Myron, *History of Nevada*, p. 674; Drury, Wells, *An Editor on the Comstock Lode*, p. 141.
2. Angel, Myron, *op. cit.*, p. 643.

## Truth and the Indian    (pp. 76–81)

1. De Quille, Dan, *The Big Bonanza*, p. 291; Mrs. M. M. Mathews, *Ten Years in Nevada*, p. 224.
2. De Quille, *op. cit.*, p. 292.
3. *Ibid.*, p. 196.
4. Davis, Sam, *The History of Nevada*, Vol. I, p. 109.
5. *Territorial Enterprise*, April 4, 1878, p. 3.
6. *Virginia Evening Chronicle*, February 12, 1879, p. 3.
7. Davis pays a very touching tribute to Captain Bob in Duncan Emrich, ed., *Comstock Bonanza*, pp. 296–303.

## The Quick and the Dead    (pp. 84–87)

1. *Virginia Evening Chronicle*, January 18, 1879, p. 3.

## "Let's Go to the Fire!"    (pp. 90–95)

1. See the Los Angeles *Times*, November 15, 1942, pp. 15, 26.
2. San Francisco *Chronicle*, October 27, 1875, p. 3; October 28, p. 3. A little group of ten or twenty men knew only too well how fast the fire moved. They were prisoners in the courthouse jail. When the fire began, they were herded from danger by the worried sheriff only to have one refuge after another gobbled by the flames. For part of the time, they were locked up in the old Sierra Nevada tunnel, not far from the flaming Ophir. For a brief time, they were even put on parole, but by nightfall were prisoners again in the Pacific Brewery—in just what section the story does not say, but we may assume it was not one of the storage rooms.
3. Smith, Grant H., *The History of the Comstock Lode*, p. 192.
4. Smith, *loc. cit.* Mackay kept his word. The old church dynamited by his men had cost $40,000 in 1868. The new, for which he is said to have provided most if not all of the financing, cost $60,000 and is even more beautiful than its predecessor. With its exquisite polished wood interior and superior Gothic design, it stands still glorious today amid a drab and dusty scene.
5. Galloway, John Debo, *Early Engineering Works Contributory to the Comstock*, p. 17.
6. Mathews, Mrs. M. M., *op. cit.*, pp. 182–83.
7. De Quille, Dan, *op. cit.*, p. 435.

## Hooray for the Fourth!    (pp. 98–103)

1. *Territorial Enterprise*, May 12, 1878, p. 3.
2. *Ibid.*, July 2, 1878, p. 3.
3. *Ibid.*, June 26, 1878, p. 3.
4. *Ibid.*, July 6, 1878, p. 3.
5. *Territorial Enterprise, loc. cit.*
6. Emrich, Duncan, ed., *Comstock Bonanza*, pp. 296–97, "Sage Brush Chief."

## "Who's Goin' Swimmin'?"  (pp. 106–111)

1. *Territorial Enterprise*, March 16, 1876, p. 3; de Quille, Dan, *op. cit.*, pp. 196, 209.
2. *Territorial Enterprise*, January 23, 1878, p. 3.


## The Strenuous Life of the Dumps  (pp. 114–119)

1. Galloway, John Debo, *op. cit.*, p. 24.
2. Michelson, Miriam, *The Wonderland of Silver and Gold*, pp. 314–15.
3. *Territorial Enterprise*, December 17, 1878, p. 3.
4. *Ibid.*, December 27, 1878, p. 3.
5. *Ibid.*, January 6, 1878, p. 3.
6. *Virginia Evening Chronicle*, September 9, 1878, p. 3; *Territorial Enterprise*, January 6, 1878, p. 3.
7. Michelson, Miriam, *loc. cit.*, *Virginia Evening Chronicle*, December 31, 1878, p. 3.
8. Mahoney, Denis J., *op. cit.*, p. 27.


## "Ho, for Treadway's!"  (pp. 122–128)

1. *Territorial Enterprise*, May 28, 1878, p. 3.
2. *Ibid.*, August 28, 1878, p. 3.


## Taking a Chance  (pp. 130–137)

1. Galloway, John Debo, *op. cit.*, p. 19.
2. King, Joseph L., *History of the San Francisco Stock Exchange and Board*, pp. 67–69.
3. San Francisco *Alta*, November 9, 1877, p. 1.
4. *Ibid.*, November 13, 1877, p. 1.
5. *Territorial Enterprise*, August 2, 1878, p. 3; August 9, p. 3.
6. *Ibid.*, August 29, 1878, p. 3.
7. *Ibid.*, December 15, 1878, p. 3.
8. Smith, Grant H., *op. cit.*, p. 222.


## When the Circus Came to Town  (pp. 140–145)

1. *Territorial Enterprise*, April 23, 1878, p. 3.
2. *Dictionary of American Biography* (New York, 1931), p. 536; Robert E. Sherwood, *Hold Yer Hosses!*, p. 37.
3. *Dictionary of American Biography*, p. 522.
4. *Virginia Evening Chronicle*, June 19, 1879, p. 3.
5. *Ibid.*, June 6, 1879, p. 3.

## Almost An Actor   (pp. 148–142)

1. Hartnoll, J. L., *Oxford Companion to the Theatre*, pp. 35–37, 40.
2. *Ibid.*, p. 834; James Coad and T. V. Mins, *Pageant of America*, Vol. XIV, p. 200.
3. *Chambers Biographical Dictionary*, pp. 23, 309.
4. Smith, *op. cit.*, p. 28; *Territorial Enterprise*, Jan. 11, 24, 1878.
5. Galloway, *op. cit.*, p. 17.
6. Gagey, Edmond M., *The San Francisco Stage*, pp. 136, 180; Coad and Mins, *op, cit.*, p. 231; Hartnoll, *op. cit.*, p. 411.
7. Hartnoll, *op. cit.*, p. 177.
8. *Ibid.*, p. 834.

## Heroes, Two for a Dime   (pp. 154–158)

1. Letter from Robert H. Hand, General Reference and Bibliography Division, Library of Congress, July 6, 1962.
2. Hayes, John Alexander, *Catalog of Dime Novel Materials*, p. 24.
3. Bragin, Charles, *Dime Novels Bibliography, 1860–1928*, p. 74.
4. *Territorial Enterprise*, Feb. 4, 1870.

## Back to the Old Home   (pp. 170–176)

1. *Virginia Evening Chronicle*, March 3, 1879, p. 3; *Mining and Scientific Press* (San Francisco), March 8, 1879, p. 152.
2. *Virginia Evening Chronicle*, July 13, 1880, p. 3.

## L'Envoi   (pp. 180–187)

1. *Virginia Evening Chronicle,* March 10, 1910.
2. *Territorial Enterprise*, May 16, 1878, p. 3; August 13, p. 3.
3. *Ibid.*, February 26, 1878, p. 3.
4. *Ibid.*, February 12, 1878, p. 3.
5. *Ibid.*, December 4, 1878, p. 3.
6. *Virginia Evening Chronicle*, May 31, 1879, p. 3.
7. *Territorial Enterprise*, July 3, 1878, p. 3; December 15, p. 3.
8. San Francisco *Examiner*, March 19, 1893, p. 18.

# A Comstock Reading List

Addenbrooke, Alice N.: *The Mistress of the Mansion* (Palo Alto, 1950).

Angel, Myron: *History of Nevada* (Oakland, 1882; Berkeley, 1958).

Bean, Walton: *Boss Ruef's San Francisco* (Berkeley, 1952).

Beebe, Lucius and Charles Clegg: *Legends of the Comstock Lode* (Oakland, 1950).

————: *U.S. West, the Saga of Wells Fargo* (New York, 1949).

————: *Virginia & Truckee* (Oakland, 1949).

Carmody, John M.: *Nevada* (The American Guide Series, Federal Works Administration; Reno, 1940).

Davis, Sam P.: *The History of Nevada* (Two vols., Reno, 1913).

De Quille, Dan: *The Big Bonanza* (New York, 1947). Originally published in 1876 as *History of the Big Bonanza.*

Drury, Wells: *An Editor on the Comstock Lode* (Palo Alto, 1948).

Duffus, R. L., *The Tower of Jewels* (New York, 1960).

Duke, Thomas S.: *Celebrated Criminal Cases of America* (San Francisco, 1910).

Emrich, Duncan, ed.: *Comstock Bonanza* (New York, 1950).

Gagey, Edmond M.: *The San Francisco Stage* (New York, 1950).

Galloway, John Debo: *Early Engineering Works Contributory to the Comstock* (Nevada Bureau of Mines, University of Nevada; Reno, 1947).

Gilbert, Benjamin Franklin: *Pioneers for 100 Years: San Jose State College, 1857–1957* (San Jose, 1957).

Glasscock, C. B.: *The Big Bonanza* (Indianapolis, 1931).

Gorham, Harry M.: *My Memories of the Comstock* (Los Angeles, 1939).

Hichborn, Franklin: *The System, as Uncovered by the San Francisco Graft Prosecution* (San Francisco, 1915).

Jensen, Vernon H.: *Heritage of Conflict* (Ithaca, New York, 1950).

King, Joseph L.: *History of the San Francisco Stock Exchange and Board* (San Francisco, 1910).

Kneiss, Gilbert H.: *Bonanza Railroads* (Stanford, 1946).

Knittle, Walter Allen: *The Early Eighteenth Century Palatine Emigration* (Philadelphia, 1936).

Lewis, Oscar: *Silver Kings* (New York, 1947).

Lillard, Richard G.: *Desert Challenge* (New York, 1942).

Lord, Eliot: *Comstock Mining and Miners* (Washington, D.C., 1883; Berkeley, 1959).

Mack, Effie M.: *History of Nevada* (Glendale, 1936).

Mahoney, Denis J.: *The Great Comstock Lode Digest from 1859–1937* (Reno, 1937).

Mapes, Gloria Millicent, Maude Sawin Taylor, Ella Knowles Gottschalk, Harriet Gaddis Spann: *Bowers Mansion* (Reno, 1952).

Marye, George Thomas, Jr.: *From '49 to '83 in California and Nevada* (San Francisco, 1923).

Mathews, Mary McNair: *Ten Years in Nevada* (Buffalo, 1880).

Michelson, Miriam: *The Wonderlode of Silver and Gold* (Boston, 1934).

Myrick, David F.: *Railroads of Nevada and Eastern California* (Berkeley, 1962).

Older, Fremont: *My Own Story* (Oakland, 1925).

Sherwood, Robert E.: *Hold Yer Hosses! The Elephants are Coming* (New York, 1932).

Shinn, Charles Howard: *The Story of the Mine* (New York, 1903).

Slayton, Asa W.: *History of the*

*Slayton Family* (Grand Rapids, Michigan, 1898).

Smith, Grant H.: *The History of the Comstock Lode, 1850–1920* (Reno, 1943).

Twain, Mark: *Roughing It* (New York, 1913).

Wagner, Jack R.: "Sagebrush Shortline" (*Railroad Magazine*, June 11, 1945).

Weir, Jeanne Elizabeth: *Nevada* (American Guide Series, Portland, Oregon, 1940).

Wells, Evelyn: *Fremont Older* (New York, 1936).

Wren, Thomas, ed.: *A History of the State of Nevada, Resources and People* (New York, 1904).

Young, John P.: *Journalism in California* (San Francisco, 1915).

# Picture Credits

BANCROFT LIBRARY: Pages 36, 38, 39, 47, 56, 57, 58, 74, 112, 129, 139, 147, 160, 178–179.

CALIFORNIA HISTORICAL SOCIETY: Pages 48, 67, 88, 89, 105, 120, 159.

DENVER PUBLIC LIBRARY, *Western Collection:* Page 121.

GRAHAME HARDY COLLECTION: Pages 83, 96.

J. S. HOLLIDAY: Pages 66, 138.

NEVADA HISTORICAL SOCIETY: Pages 97, 104.

OAKLAND MUSEUM: Pages 49, 59, 82, 153, 169.

PATRICIA McCARTHY: Page 113.

SOCIETY OF CALIFORNIA PIONEERS: Pages 146, 161.

WELLS FARGO BANK HISTORY ROOM: Pages 37, 177.

# INDEX

*The text for this book was set in Century
Schoolbook by George Banta Company, Inc.,
Menasha, Wisconsin, who did also the printing
and binding. The paper is Hilding Hi-Bulk,
cream white. The cloth is Columbia
Mill's Renne, natural finish.*

*Design by John Beyer.*